CAMBRIDGE LIBRARY COLLECTION

Books of enduring scholarly value

English Men of Letters

In the 1870s, Macmillan publishers began to issue a series of books called 'English Men of Letters' – biographies of English writers by other English writers. The general editor of the series was the journalist, critic, politician, and supporter (and later biographer) of Gladstone, John Morley (1838–1923). The aim was to provide a short introduction to each subject and his works, but also that the life should illuminate the works, and vice versa. The subjects range chronologically from Chaucer to Thackeray and Dickens, and an important feature of the series is that many of the authors (Henry James on Hawthorne, Ward on Dickens) were discussing writers of the previous generation, and some (Trollope on Thackeray) had even known their subjects personally. The series exemplifies the British approach to literary biography and criticism at the end of the nineteenth century, and also reveals which authors were at that time regarded as canonical.

Chaucer

This biography of Geoffrey Chaucer (*c.* 1340–1400) was published in the first series of English Men of Letters in 1879. Its author, Sir Adolphus William Ward (1837–1924), a prominent scholar who became President of the British Academy, wrote on English literature from the sixteenth to the nineteenth centuries, translated Curtius' *History of Greece*, and was a historian of both Britain and Germany. He approached the task of writing Chaucer's life as a historian rather than as a literary critic, emphasising the archival sources from which information on Chaucer the man, the civil servant and the courtier could be drawn, and placing the life very much in the context of the times. An epilogue discusses the legacy of the 'father of English poetry' to the poets and dramatists of the sixteenth and seventeenth centuries, and the renewal of interest in Chaucer's works in the nineteenth century.

T0371079

Cambridge University Press has long been a pioneer in the reissuing of out-of-print titles from its own backlist, producing digital reprints of books that are still sought after by scholars and students but could not be reprinted economically using traditional technology. The Cambridge Library Collection extends this activity to a wider range of books which are still of importance to researchers and professionals, either for the source material they contain, or as landmarks in the history of their academic discipline.

Drawing from the world-renowned collections in the Cambridge University Library, and guided by the advice of experts in each subject area, Cambridge University Press is using state-of-the-art scanning machines in its own Printing House to capture the content of each book selected for inclusion. The files are processed to give a consistently clear, crisp image, and the books finished to the high quality standard for which the Press is recognised around the world. The latest print-on-demand technology ensures that the books will remain available indefinitely, and that orders for single or multiple copies can quickly be supplied.

The Cambridge Library Collection will bring back to life books of enduring scholarly value (including out-of-copyright works originally issued by other publishers) across a wide range of disciplines in the humanities and social sciences and in science and technology.

Chaucer

Adolphus William Ward

CAMBRIDGE
UNIVERSITY PRESS

CAMBRIDGE UNIVERSITY PRESS

Cambridge, New York, Melbourne, Madrid, Cape Town,
Singapore, São Paolo, Delhi, Tokyo, Mexico City

Published in the United States of America by Cambridge University Press, New York

www.cambridge.org
Information on this title: www.cambridge.org/9781108034647

© in this compilation Cambridge University Press 2011

This edition first published 1879
This digitally printed version 2011

ISBN 978-1-108-03464-7 Paperback

English Men of Letters

EDITED BY JOHN MORLEY

CHAUCER

CHAUCER

BY

ADOLPHUS WILLIAM WARD

London:

MACMILLAN AND CO.

1879.

NOTE.

THE peculiar conditions of this essay must be left to explain themselves. It could not have been written at all without the aid of the Publications of the Chaucer Society, and more especially of the labours of the Society's Director, Mr. Furnivall. To other recent writers on Chaucer—including Mr. Fleay, from whom I never differ but with hesitation—I have referred, in so far as it was in my power to do so. Perhaps I may take this opportunity of expressing a wish that Pauli's *History of England*, a work beyond the compliment of an acknowledgment, were accessible to every English reader.

A. W. W.

CONTENTS.

CHAUCER.

CHAPTER I.

THE biography of Geoffrey Chaucer is no longer a mixture
of unsifted facts, and of more or less hazardous conjectures. Many and wide as are the gaps in our knowledge
concerning the course of his outer life, and doubtful as many
important passages of it remain—in vexatious contrast
with the certainty of other relatively insignificant *data*—
we have at least become aware of the foundations on
which alone a trustworthy account of it can be built.
These foundations consist partly of a meagre though
gradually increasing array of external evidence, chiefly to
be found in public documents,—in the Royal Wardrobe
Book, the Issue Rolls of the Exchequer, the Customs
Rolls, and suchlike records—partly of the conclusions
which may be drawn with confidence from the internal
evidence of the poet's own indisputably genuine works,
together with a few references to him in the writings of
his contemporaries or immediate successors. Which of
his works are to be accepted as genuine, necessarily forms
the subject of an antecedent enquiry, such as cannot with

B

any degree of safety be conducted except on principles
far from infallible with regard to all the instances to
which they have been applied, but now accepted by
the large majority of competent scholars.   Thus, by
a process which is in truth dulness and dryness itself
except to patient endeavour stimulated by the enthusiasm
of special literary research, a limited number of results has
been safely established, and others have at all events been
placed beyond reasonable doubt.   Around a third series
of conclusions or conjectures the tempest of controversy
still rages; and even now it needs a wary step to pass
without fruitless deviations through a maze of assumptions consecrated by their longevity, or commended to
sympathy by the fervour of personal conviction.

A single instance must suffice to indicate both the
difficulty and the significance of many of those questions
of Chaucerian biography which, whether interesting or
not in themselves, have to be determined before Chaucer's
life can be written.   They are not " all and some " mere
antiquarians' puzzles, of interest only to those who have
leisure and inclination for microscopic enquiries.   So
with the point immediately in view.   It has been said
with much force that Tyrwhitt, whose services to the
study of Chaucer remain uneclipsed by those of any
other scholar, would have composed a quite different
biography of the poet, had he not been confounded by
the formerly (and here and there still) accepted date of
Chaucer's birth, the year 1328.   For the correctness of
this date Tyrwhitt " supposed " the poet's tombstone in
Westminster Abbey to be the voucher; but the slab
placed on a pillar near his grave (it is said at the desire of
Caxton), appears to have therely borne a Latin inscription
without any dates; and the marble monument erected in

its stead "in the name of the Muses" by Nicolas
Brigham in 1556, while giving October 25th, 1400, as the
day of Chaucer's death, makes no mention either of the
date of his birth or of the number of years to which he
attained, and, indeed, promises no more information than
it gives. That Chaucer's contemporary, the poet Gower,
should have referred to him in the year 1392 as "now in
his days old," is at best a very vague sort of testimony,
more especially as it is by mere conjecture that the year
of Gower's own birth is placed as far back as 1320. Still
less weight can be attached to the circumstance that
another poet, Occleve, who clearly regarded himself as
the disciple of one by many years his senior, in
accordance with the common phraseology of his (and,
indeed, of other) times, spoke of the older writer as
his "father" and "father reverent." In a coloured
portrait carefully painted from memory by Occleve on
the margin of a manuscript, Chaucer is represented
with grey hair and beard; but this could not of itself
be taken to contradict the supposition that he died about
the age of sixty. And Leland's assertion that Chaucer
attained to old age self-evidently rests on tradition
only; for Leland was born more than a century after
Chaucer died. Nothing occurring in any of Chaucer's
own works of undisputed genuineness throws any real
light on the subject. His poem, the *House of Fame*,
has been variously dated; but at any period of his
manhood he might have said, as he says there, that he
was "too old" to learn astronomy, and preferred to take
his science on faith. In the curious lines called *L'Envoy
de Chaucer à Scogan*, the poet, while blaming his friend
for his want of perseverance in a love-suit, classes himself
among "them that be hoar and round of shape," and

speaks of himself and his Muse as out of date and rusty. But there seems no sufficient reason for removing the date of the composition of these lines to an earlier year than 1393 ; and poets as well as other men since Chaucer have spoken of themselves as old and obsolete at fifty. A similar remark might be made concerning the reference to the poet's old age "which dulleth him in his spirit," in the *Complaint of Venus*, generally ascribed to the last decennium of Chaucer's life. If we reject the evidence of a further passage, in the *Cuckoo and the Nightingale*, a poem of disputed genuineness, we accordingly arrive at the conclusion that there is no reason for demurring to the only direct external evidence in existence as to the date of Chaucer's birth. At a famous trial of a cause of chivalry held at Westminster in 1386, Chaucer, who had gone through part of a campaign with one of the litigants, appeared as a witness ; and on this occasion his age was, doubtless on his own deposition, recorded as that of a man "of forty years and upwards," who had borne arms for twenty-seven years. A careful enquiry into the accuracy of the record as to the ages of the numerous other witnesses at the same trial has established it in an overwhelming majority of instances ; and it is absurd gratuitously to charge Chaucer with having understated his age from motives of vanity. The conclusion, there-fore, seems to remain unshaken, that he was born about the year 1340, or some time between that year and 1345.

Now, we possess a charming poem by Chaucer called the *Assembly of Fowls*, elaborately courtly in its concep-tion, and in its execution giving proofs of Italian reading on the part of its author, as well as of a ripe humour such as is rarely an accompaniment of extreme youth.

This poem has been thought by earlier commentators to allegorise an event known to have happened in 1358, by later critics another which occurred in 1364. Clearly, the assumption that the period from 1340 to 1345 includes the date of Chaucer's birth, suffices of itself to stamp the one of these conjectures as untenable, and the other as improbable, and (when the style of the poem and treatment of its subject are taken into account) adds weight to the other reasons in favour of the date 1381 for the poem in question. Thus, backwards and forwards, the disputed points in Chaucer's biography and the question of his works are affected by one another.

Chaucer's life, then, spans rather more than the latter half of the fourteenth century, the last year of which was indisputably the year of his death. In other words, it covers rather more than the interval between the most glorious epoch of Edward III.'s reign—for Crecy was fought in 1346—and the downfall, in 1399, of his unfortunate successor Richard II.

The England of this period was but a little land, if numbers be the test of greatness; but in Edward III.'s time as in that of Henry V., who inherited so much of Edward's policy and revived so much of his glory, there stirred in this little body a mighty heart. It is only of a small population that the author of the *Vision concerning Piers Plowman* could have gathered the representatives into a single field, or that Chaucer himself could have composed a family picture fairly comprehending, though not altogether exhausting, the chief national character-types. In the year of King Richard II.'s accession (1377), according to a trustworthy calculation based

upon the result of that year's poll-tax, the total number
of the inhabitants of England seems to have been two
millions and a half. A quarter of a century earlier—in
the days of Chaucer's boyhood—their numbers had been
perhaps twice as large. For not less than four great pestilences (in 1348–9, 1361–2, 1369, and 1375–6) had
swept over the land, and at least one-half of its population,
including two-thirds of the inhabitants of the capital, had
been carried off by the ravages of the obstinate epidemic—
"the foul death of England," as it was called in a formula
of execration in use among the people. In this year 1377,
London, where Chaucer was doubtless born as well as
bred, where the greater part of his life was spent, and
where the memory of his name is one of those associations which seem familiarly to haunt the banks of the
historic river from Thames Street to Westminster, apparently numbered not more than 35,000 souls. But if,
from the nature of the case, no place was more exposed
than London to the inroads of the Black Death, neither
was any other so likely elastically to recover from them.
For the reign of Edward III. had witnessed a momentous
advance in the prosperity of the capital,—an advance re-
flecting itself in the outward changes introduced during
the same period into the architecture of the city. Its
wealth had grown larger as its houses had grown higher ;
and mediæval London, such as we are apt to picture it to
ourselves, seems to have derived those leading features
which it so long retained, from the days when Chaucer,
with downcast but very observant eyes, passed along its
streets between Billingsgate and Aldgate. Still, here as
elsewhere in England the remembrance of the most awful
physical visitations which have ever befallen the country
must have long lingered ; and, after all has been said, it is

wonderful that the traces of them should be so exceedingly
scanty in Chaucer's pages. Twice only in his poems does
he refer to the Plague :—once in an allegorical fiction
which is of Italian if not of French origin, and where,
therefore, no special reference to the ravages of the disease
in England may be intended when Death is said to have
" a thousand slain this pestilence,"—

> he hath slain this year
> Hence over a mile, within a great villáge
> Both men and women, child and hind and page.

The other allusion is a more than half humorous one. It
occurs in the description of the *Doctor of Physic*, the
grave graduate in purple surcoat and blue white-furred
hood; nor, by the way, may this portrait itself be altogether without its use as throwing some light on the helplessness of fourteenth-century medical science. For though
in all the world there was none like this doctor to *speak* of
physic and of surgery ;—though he was a very perfect practitioner, and never at a loss for telling the cause of any
malady and for supplying the patient with the appropriate
drug, sent in by the doctor's old and faithful friends the
apothecaries ;—though he was well versed in all the authorities from Æsculapius to the writer of the *Rosa Anglica*
(who cures inflammation homœopathically by the use of
red draperies) ;—though like a truly wise physician he
began at home by caring anxiously for his own digestion
and for his peace of mind ("his study was but little in
the Bible ") :—yet the basis of his scientific knowledge
was " astronomy," i. e. astrology, " the better part of
medicine," as Roger Bacon calls it; together with that
" natural magic " by which, as Chaucer elsewhere tells us,
the famous among the learned have known how to make

men whole or sick.   And there was one specific which,
from a double point of view, Chaucer's Doctor of Physic
esteemed very highly, and was loth to part with on
frivolous pretexts.   He was but easy (i. e. slack) of
" dispence : "—

> He keptë that he won in pestilence.
> For gold in physic is a cordial;
> Therefore he lovèd gold in speciál.

Meanwhile the ruling classes seem to have been left
untouched in heart by these successive ill-met and ill-
guarded trials, which had first smitten the lower orders
chiefly, then the higher with the lower (if the Plague of
1349 had swept off an archbishop, that of 1361 struck
down among others Henry Duke of Lancaster, the father
of Chaucer's Duchess Blanche).   Calamities such as these
would assuredly have been treated as warnings sent
from on high, both in earlier times, when a Church
better braced for the due performance of its never-ending
task, eagerly interpreted to awful ears the signs of the wrath
of God, and by a later generation, leavened in spirit
by the self-searching morality of Puritanism.   But from
the sorely-tried third quarter of the fourteenth century
the solitary voice of Langland cries, as the voice of Conscience preaching with her cross, that " these pestilences "
are the penalty of sin and of naught else.   It is assuredly
presumptuous for one generation, without the fullest
proof, to accuse another of thoughtlessness or heartless-
ness ; and though the classes for which Chaucer mainly
wrote and with which he mainly felt, were in all probability as little inclined to improve the occasions of the
Black Death as the middle classes of the present day
would be to fall on their knees after a season of com-

mercial ruin, yet signs are not wanting that in the later years of the fourteenth century words of admonition came to be not unfrequently spoken. The portents of the eventful year 1382 called forth moralisings in English verse, and the pestilence of 1391 a rhymed lamentation in Latin ; and at different dates in King Richard's reign the poet Gower, Chaucer's contemporary and friend, inveighed both in Latin and in English, from his conservative point of view, against the corruption and sinfulness of society at large. But by this time the great peasant insurrection had added its warning, to which it was impossible to remain deaf.

A self-confident nation, however, is slow to betake itself to sackcloth and ashes. On the whole it is clear, that though the last years of Edward III. were a season of failure and disappointment,—though from the period of the First Pestilence onwards the signs increase of the king's unpopularity and of the people's discontent,—yet the overburdened and enfeebled nation was brought almost as slowly as the King himself to renounce the proud position of a conquering power. In 1363 he had celebrated the completion of his fiftieth year ; and three suppliant kings had at that time been gathered as satellites round the sun of his success. By 1371 he had lost all his allies, and nearly all the conquests gained by himself and the valiant Prince of Wales ; and during the years remaining to him his subjects hated his rule and angrily assailed his favourites. From being a conquering power the English monarchy was fast sinking into an island which found it difficult to defend its own shores. There were times towards the close of Edward's and early in his successor's reign, when matters would have gone hard with English traders, naturally desirous of having their money's worth for their subsidy

of tonnage and poundage, and anxious, like their type the
Merchant in Chaucer, that "the sea were kept for anything" between Middelburgh and Harwich, had not some
of them, such as the Londoner John Philpot, occasionally
armed and manned a squadron of ships on their own
account, in defiance of red tape and its censures. But
in the days when Chaucer and the generation with which
he grew up were young, the ardour of foreign conquest
had not yet died out in the land, and clergy and laity
cheerfully co-operated in bearing the burdens which military glory has at all times brought with it for a civilised
people. The high spirit of the English nation, at a time
when the decline in its fortunes was already near at hand
(1366), is evident from the answer given to the application
from Rome for the arrears of thirty-three years of the
tribute promised by King John, or rather from what must
unmistakeably have been the drift of that answer. Its
terms are unknown, but the demand was never afterwards repeated.

The power of England in the period of an ascendancy
to which she so tenaciously sought to cling, had not been
based only upon the valour of her arms. Our country was
already a rich one in comparison with most others in
Europe. Other purposes besides that of providing good
cheer for a robust generation were served by the wealth
of her great landed proprietors, and of the "worthy
vavasours" (smaller landowners) who, like. Chaucer's
Franklin—a very Saint Julian or pattern of hospitality—
knew not what it was to be "without baked meat in the
house," where their

> tables dormant in the hall alway
> Stood ready covered all the longë day.

From this source, and from the well-filled coffers of the

traders came the laity's share of the expenses of those
foreign wars which did so much to consolidate national
feeling in England.   The foreign companies of merchants
long contrived to retain the chief share of the banking
business and export trade assigned to them by the short-
sighted commercial policy of Edward III., and the weaving
and fishing industries of Hanseatic and Flemish immi-
grants had established an almost unbearable competition
in our own ports and towns.   But the active import trade,
which already connected England with both nearer and
remoter parts of Christendom, must have been largely in
native hands; and English chivalry, diplomacy, and
literature followed in the lines of the trade-routes to the
Baltic and the Mediterranean.   Our mariners, like their
type the *Shipman* in Chaucer (an anticipation of the
" Venturer " of later days, with the pirate as yet, perhaps,
more strongly marked in him than the patriot),—

> knew well all the havens, as they were
> From Gothland, to the Cape of Finisterre,
> And every creek in Brittany and Spain.

Doubtless, as may be noticed in passing, much of the
tendency on the part of our shipmen in this period to self-
help in offence as well as in defence, was due to the fact
that the mercantile navy was frequently employed in
expeditions of war, vessels and men being at times seized
or impressed for the purpose by order of the Crown.   On
one of these occasions the port of Dartmouth, whence
Chaucer at a venture ("for aught I wot") makes his
Shipman hail, is found contributing a larger total of ships
and men than any other port in England.   For the rest,
Flanders was certainly still far ahead of her future rival in
wealth, and in mercantile and industrial activity; as a

manufacturing country she had no equal, and in trade the
rival she chiefly feared was still the German Hansa.
Chaucer's *Merchant* characteristically wears a "Flandrish
beaver hat;" and it is no accident that the scene of the
Pardoner's Tale, which begins with a description of
"superfluity abominable," is laid in Flanders. In England,
indeed the towns never came to domineer as they did in
the Netherlands.   Yet, since no trading country will long
submit to be ruled by the landed interest only, so in proportion as the English towns, and London especially,
grew richer, their voices were listened to in the settlement
of the affairs of the nation.   It might be very well for
Chaucer to close the description of his *Merchant* with
what looks very much like a fashionable writer's half
sneer :—

> Forsooth, he was a worthy man withal;
> But, truly, I wot nót how men him call.

Yet not only was high political and social rank reached
by individual "merchant princes," such as the wealthy
William de la Pole, a descendant of whom is said (though
on unsatisfactory evidence) to have been Chaucer's grand-
daughter, but the government of the country came to be
very perceptibly influenced by the class from which they
sprang.   On the accession of Richard II., two London
citizens were appointed controllers of the war-subsidies
granted to the Crown; and in the Parliament of 1382
a committee of fourteen merchants refused to entertain
the question of a merchants' loan to the king.   The
importance and self-consciousness of the smaller tradesmen
and handicraftsmen increased with that of the great
merchants.   When in 1393 King Richard II. marked the
termination of his quarrel with the City of London by a
stately procession through "new Troy," he was welcomed,

according to the Friar who has commemorated the event
in Latin verse, by the trades in an array resembling an
angelic host; and among the crafts enumerated we recognise several of those represented in Chaucer's company
of pilgrims—by the *Carpenter*, the *Webbe* (Weaver), and
the *Dyer*, all clothed

> in one livery
> Of a solémn and great fraternity.

The middle class, in short, was learning to hold up its
head, collectively and individually. The historical original
of Chaucer's *Host*—the actual Master Harry Bailly, vintner
and landlord of the Tabard Inn in Southwark, was likewise a member of Parliament, and very probably felt as
sure of himself in real life as the mimic personage bearing
his name does in its fictitious reproduction. And he and
his fellows, the "poor and simple Commons"—for so
humble was the style they were wont to assume in their
addresses to the sovereign,—began to look upon themselves,
and to be looked upon, as a power in the State. The
London traders and handicraftsmen knew what it was to
be well-to-do citizens, and if they had failed to understand it, home monition would have helped to make it
clear to them :—

> Well seeméd each of them a fair burgéss,
> For sitting in a guildhall on a dais.
> And each one for the wisdom that he can
> Was shapely for to be an alderman.
> They had enough of chattels and of rent,
> And very gladly would their wives assent;
> And, truly, else they had been much to blame.
> It is full fair to be yclept *madáme*,
> And fair to go to vigils all before,
> And have a mantle royally y-bore.

The English State had ceased to be the feudal monarchy

—the ramification of contributory courts and camps—of
the crude days of William the Conqueror and his successors. The Norman lords and their English dependants no
longer formed two separate elements in the body politic. In
the great French wars of Edward III., the English armies
had no longer mainly consisted of the baronial levies. The
nobles had indeed, as of old, ridden into battle at the
head of their vassals and retainers; but the body of the
force had been made up of Englishmen serving for pay,
and armed with their national implement, the bow—such
as Chaucer's *Yeoman* carried with him on the ride to
Canterbury :—

> A sheaf of peacock arrows bright and keen
> Under his belt he bare full thriftily.
> Well could he dress his tackle yeomanly :
> His arrows droopèd not with feathers low,
> And in his hand he bare a mighty bow.

The use of the bow was specially favoured by both
Edward III. and his successor; and when early in the
next century the chivalrous Scottish king, James I. (of
whom mention will be made among Chaucer's poetic
disciples) returned from his long English captivity to his
native land, he had no more eager care than that his subjects should learn to emulate the English in the handling
of their favourite weapon. Chaucer seems to be unable
to picture an army without it, and we find him relating
how, from ancient Troy,—

> Hector and many a worthy wight out went
> With spear in hand, and with their big bows bent.

No wonder that when the battles were fought by the
people itself, and when the cost of the wars was to so large
an extent defrayed by its self-imposed contributions, the

Scottish and French campaigns should have called forth that national enthusiasm which found an echo in the songs of Lawrence Minot, as hearty war-poetry as has been composed in any age of our literature. They were put forth in 1352, and considering the unusual popularity they are said to have enjoyed, it is not impossible that they may have reached Chaucer's ears in his boyhood.

Before the final collapse of the great King's fortunes, and his death in a dishonoured old age, the ambition of his heir, the proudest hope of both dynasty and nation, had overleapt itself, and the Black Prince had preceded his father to the tomb. The good ship England (so sang a contemporary poet) was left without rudder or helm ; and in a kingdom full of faction and discontent the future of the Plantagenet throne depended on a child. While the young king's ambitious uncle, John of Gaunt, Duke of Lancaster (Chaucer's patron), was in nominal retirement, and his academical ally, Wyclif, was gaining popularity as the mouthpiece of the resistance to the papal demands, there were fermenting beneath the surface elements of popular agitation, which had been but little taken into account by the political factions of Edward the Third's reign, and by that part of its society with which Chaucer was more especially connected   But the multitude, whose turn in truth comes but rarely in the history of a nation, must every now and then make itself heard, although poets may seem all but blind and deaf to the tempest as it rises, and bursts, and passes away. Many causes had concurred to excite the insurrection which temporarily destroyed the influence of John of Gaunt, and which for long cast a deep shade upon the effects of the teaching of Wyclif. The acquisition of a measure of rights and power by the middle classes had caused a general swaying

upwards ; and throughout the peoples of Europe floated
those dreams and speculations concerning the equality
and fraternity of all men, which needed but a stimulus
and an opportunity to assume the practical shape of a
revolution. The melancholy thought which pervades
Langland's *Vision* is still that of the helplessness of
the poor ; and the remedy to which he looks against the
corruption of the governing classes is the advent of a
superhuman king, whom he identifies with the ploughman
himself, the representative of suffering humility. But
about the same time as that of the composition of this
poem—or not long afterwards—Wyclif had sent forth
among the people his "simple priests," who illustrated by
contrast the conflict which his teaching exposed between
the existing practice of the Church and the original documents of her faith. The connexion between Wyclif's teaching and the peasants' insurrection under Richard II. is as
undeniable as that between Luther's doctrines and the great
social uprising in Germany a century and a half afterwards.
When, upon the declaration of the Papal Schism, Wyclif
abandoned all hope of a reform of the Church from within,
and, defying the injunctions of foe and friend alike, entered
upon a course of theological opposition, the popular influence of his followers must have tended to spread a
theory admitting of very easy application *ad hominem*—
the theory, namely, that the tenure of all offices, whether
spiritual or temporal, is justified only by the personal fitness
of their occupants. With such levelling doctrine, the
Socialism of popular preachers like John Balle might seem
to coincide with sufficient closeness ; and since worthiness
was not to be found in the holders of either spiritual or temporal authority, of either ecclesiastical or lay wealth, the
time had palpably come for the poor man to enjoy his

own again. Then, the advent of a weak government, over
which a powerful kinsman of the king and unconcealed
adversary of the Church was really seeking to recover the
control, and the imposition of a tax coming home to all men
except actual beggars, and filling serfdom's cup of bitterness
to overflowing, supplied the opportunity, and the insurrection broke out. Its violence fell short of that of the
French *Jacquerie* a quarter of a century earlier; but no
doubt could exist as to its critical importance. As it
happened, the revolt turned with special fury against the
possessions of the Duke of Lancaster, whose sympathies
with the cause of ecclesiastical reform it definitively extinguished.

After the suppression of this appalling movement by a
party of Order comprehending in it all who had anything
to lose, a period of reaction ensued. In the reign of
Richard II., whichever faction might be in the ascendant,
and whatever direction the king's own sympathies may
have originally taken, the last state of the peasantry was
without doubt worse than the first. Wycliffism as an
influence rapidly declined with the death of Wyclif himself, as it hardly could but decline, considering the
absence from his teaching of any tangible system of
church government; and Lollardry came to be the
popular name, or nickname, for any and every form of
dissent from the existing system. Finally, Henry of
Lancaster, John of Gaunt's son, mounted the throne as
a sort of saviour of society,—a favourite character for
usurpers to pose in before the applauding assemblage of
those who claim "a stake in the country." Chaucer's
contemporary, Gower, whose wisdom was of the kind
which goes with the times, who was in turn a flatterer of
Richard and (by the simple expedient of a revised second

edition of his *magnum opus*) a flatterer of Henry, offers
better testimony than Chaucer to the conservatism of the
upper classes of his age, and to the single-minded anxiety
for the good times when

> Justice of law is held ;
> The privilege of royalty
> Is safe, and all the barony
> Worshippèd is in its estate.
> The people stands in obeisánce
> Under the rule of governánce.

Chaucer is less explicit, and may have been too little
of a politician by nature to care for preserving an outward consistency in his incidental remarks concerning the
lower classes. In his *Clerk's Tale* he finds room for a
very dubious commonplace about the "stormy people," its
levity, untruthfulness, indiscretion, fickleness, and gar-
rulity, and the folly of putting any trust in it. In his
Nun's Priest's Tale he further enlivens one of the liveliest
descriptions of a hue-and-cry ever put upon paper by a
direct reference to the Peasants' Rebellion :—

> So hideous was the noise, ah *bencité!*
> That of a truth Jack Straw, and his meinie
> Not madë never shoutës half so shrill,
> When that they any Fleming meant to kill.

Assuredly, again, there is an unmistakably conservative
tone in the *Ballad* purporting to have been sent by him
to King Richard, with its refrain as to all being "lost for
want of steadfastness," and its admonition to its sovereign
to

> . . shew forth the sword of castigatión.

On the other hand, it would be unjust to leave unnoticed
the passage, at once powerful and touching, in the so-called

Parson's Tale (the sermon which closes the *Canterbury Tales* as Chaucer left them), in which certain lords are reproached for taking of their bondmen *amercements,* "which might more reasonably be called extortions than *amercements,*" while lords in general are commanded to be good to their thralls (serfs), because "those that they clept thralls, be God's people; for humble folks be Christ's friends; they be contubernially with the Lord." The solitary type, however, of the labouring man proper which Chaucer, in manifest remembrance of Langland's allegory, produces, is one which, beautiful and affecting as it is, has in it a flavour of the comfortable sentiment, that things are as they should be. This is—not of course the *Parson* himself, of which most significant character hereafter, but—the *Parson's* brother, the *Ploughman.* He is a true labourer and a good, religious and charitable in his life,—and always ready to pay his tithes. In short, he is a true Christian, but at the same time the ideal rather than the prototype, if one may so say, of the conservative working man.

Such were some, though of course some only, of the general currents of English public life in the latter half— Chaucer's half—of the fourteenth century. Its social features were naturally in accordance with the course of the national history. In the first place, the slow and painful process of amalgamation between the Normans and the English was still unfinished, though the reign of Edward III. went far towards completing what had rapidly advanced since the reigns of John and Henry III. By the middle of the fourteenth century English had become, or was just becoming, the common tongue of the whole nation. Among the political poems and songs preserved from the days of Edward III. and Richard II.,

not a single one composed on English soil is written in
French. Parliament was opened by an English speech
in the year 1363, and in the previous year the proceedings
in the law courts were ordered to be conducted in the
native tongue. Yet when Chaucer wrote his *Canterbury
Tales*, it seems still to have continued the pedantic
affectation of a profession for its members, like Chaucer's
Man of Law, to introduce French law-terms into common
conversation; so that it is natural enough to find the
Summoner following suit, and interlarding his *Tale* with
the Latin scraps picked up by him from the decrees and
pleadings of the ecclesiastical courts. Meanwhile, mani-
fold difficulties had delayed or interfered with the fusion
between the two races, before the victory of the English
language showed this fusion to have been in substance
accomplished. One of these difficulties, which has been
sometimes regarded as fundamental, has doubtless been
exaggerated by national feeling on either side; but that
it existed is not to be denied. Already in those ages the
national character and temperament of French and English
differed largely from one another; though the reasons why
they so differed, remain a matter of argument. In a
dialogue, dated from the middle of the fourteenth century, the French interlocutor attributes this difference to
the respective national beverages : " *We* are nourished
with the pure juice of the grape, while naught but the
dregs is sold to the English, who will take anything for
liquor that is liquid." The case is put with scarcely greater
politeness by a living French critic of high repute, according to whom the English, still weighted down by Teutonic
phlegm, were drunken gluttons, agitated at intervals by
poetic enthusiasm, while the Normans, on the other hand,
lightened by their transplantation, and by the admixture

of a variety of elements, already found the claims of
esprit developing themselves within them. This is an
explanation which explains nothing—least of all, the
problem : why the lively strangers should have required
the contact with insular phlegm in order to receive the
creative impulse—why, in other words, Norman-French
literature should have derived so enormous an advantage
from the transplantation of Normans to English ground.
But the evil days when the literary labours of Englishmen had been little better than bond-service to the tastes
of their foreign masters had passed away, since the
Norman barons had, from whatever motive, invited the
commons of England to take a share with them in the
national councils. After this, the question of the relations
between the two languages, and the wider one of the
relations between the two nationalities, could only be decided by the peaceable adjustment of the influences exercised by the one side upon the other. The Norman noble,
his ideas, and the expression they found in forms of life
and literature, had henceforth, so to speak, to stand on
their merits; the days of their dominion as a matter
of course had passed away.

Together with not a little of their political power, the
Norman nobles of Chaucer's time had lost something of
the traditions of their order. Chivalry had not quite come
to an end with the Crusades ; but it was a difficult task to
maintain all its laws, written and unwritten, in these degenerate days. No laurels were any longer to be gained
in the Holy Land ; and though the campaigns of the
great German Order against the pagans of Prussia and
Lithuania attracted the service of many an English
knight—in the middle of the century, Henry, Duke of
Lancaster, fought there, as his grandson, afterwards King

Henry IV., did forty years later—yet the substitute was
hardly adequate in kind.   Of the great mediæval companies of Knights, the most famous had, early in the
century, perished under charges which were undoubtedly
in the main foul fictions, but at the same time were only
too much in accord with facts betokening an unmistakable
decay of the true spirit of chivalry ; before the century
closed, lawyers were rolling parchments in the halls of the
Templars by the Thames.   Thus, though the age of
chivalry had not yet ended, its supremacy was already
on the wane, and its ideal was growing dim.   In the
history of English chivalry the reign of Edward III. is
memorable, not only for the foundation of our most illustrious order of knighthood, but likewise for many typical
acts of knightly valour and courtesy, as well on the part
of the King when in his better days, as on that of his
heroic son.   Yet it cannot be by accident that an un-
definable air of the old-fashioned clings to that most
delightful of all Chaucer's character-sketches, the *Knight* of
the *Canterbury Tales*.   His warlike deeds at Alexandria,
in Prussia, and elsewhere, may be illustrated from those
of more than one actual knight of the times ; and the
whole description of him seems founded on one by a
French poet of King John of Bohemia, who had at least
the external features of a knight of the old school.   The
chivalry, however, which was in fashion as the century
advanced, was one outwardly far removed from the sturdy
simplicity of Chaucer's *Knight*, and inwardly often rotten
in more than one vital part.   In show and splendour
a higher point was probably reached in Edward III.'s
than in any preceding reign.   The extravagance in dress
which prevailed in this period is too well known a
characteristic of it to need dwelling upon.   Sumptuary

laws in vain sought to restrain this foible ; and it rose to such ⸜a pitch as even to oblige men, lest they should be precluded from indulging in gorgeous raiment, to abandon hospitality, a far more amiable species of excess. When the kinds of clothing respectively worn by the different classes served as distinctions of rank, the display of splendour in one class could hardly fail to provoke emulation in the others. The long-lived English love for "crying" colours shows itself amusingly enough in the early pictorial representations of several of Chaucer's Canterbury pilgrims, though in floridity of apparel, as of ſpeech, the youthful *Squire* bears away the bell :—

> Embroidered was he, as it were a mead
> All full of freshest flowers, white and red.

But of the artificiality and extravagance of the costumes of these times we have direct contemporary evidence, and loud contemporary complaints. Now, it is the jagged cut of the garments, punched and shredded by the man-milliner ; now, the wide and high collars and the long-pointed boots, which attract the indignation of the moralist ; at one time he inveighs against the "horrible disordinate scantness" of the clothing worn by gallants, at another against the "outrageous array" in which ladies love to exhibit their charms. The knights' horses are decked out with not less finery than are the knights themselves, with "curious harness, as in saddles and bridles, cruppers, and breast-plates, covered with precious clothing, and with bars and plates of gold and silver." And though it is hazardous to stigmatize the fashions of any one period as specially grotesque, yet it is significant of this age to find the reigning court beauty appearing at a tournament robed as Queen of the Sun ; while even a lady from a manufacturing

district, the *Wife of Bath*, makes the most of her opportunities to be seen as well as to see. Her "kerchiefs"
were "full fine" of texture, and weighed, one might be
sworn, ten pound—

> That on a Sunday were upon her head.
> Her hosen too were of fine scarlet red,
> Full straight y-tied, and shoes full moist and new.
>
> .   .   .   .   .   .
>
> Upon an ambler easily she sat,
> Y-wimpled well, and on her head a hat,
> As broad as is a buckler or a targe.

So, with a foot-mantle round her hips, and a pair of sharp
spurs on her feet, she looked as defiant as any self-
conscious Amazon of any period. It might perhaps be
shown how in more important artistic efforts than fashions
of dress this age displayed its aversion from simplicity and
moderation. At all events, the love of the florid and
overloaded declares itself in what we know concerning
the social life of the nobility, as, for instance, we find that
life reflected in the pages of Froissart, whose counts and
lords seem neither to clothe themselves nor to feed themselves, nor to talk, pray, or swear like ordinary mortals.
The *Vows of the Heron*, a poem of the earlier part of
King Edward III.'s reign, contains a choice collection of
strenuous knightly oaths; and in a humbler way the rest
of the population very naturally imitated the parlance of
their rulers, and in the words of the *Parson's Tale*,
"dismembered Christ by soul, heart, bones, and body."

But there is one very much more important feature to
be noticed in the social life of the nobility, for whom
Chaucer's poetry must have largely replaced the French
verse in which they had formerly delighted. The relation
between knight and lady plays a great part in the history

as well as in the literature of the later Plantagenet period ;
and incontestably its conceptions of this relation still retained much of the pure sentiment belonging to the best and
most fervent times of Christian chivalry. The highest religious expression which has ever been given to man's sense of
woman's mission, as his life's comfort and crown, was still
a universally dominant belief. To the Blessed Virgin, King
Edward III. dedicated his principal religious foundation ;
and Chaucer, to whatever extent his opinions or sentiments may have been in accordance with ideas of ecclesiastical reform, displays a pious devotion towards the
foremost Saint of the Church. The lyric entitled the
Praise of Women, in which she is enthusiastically recog-
nized as the representative of the whole of her sex, is
generally rejected as not Chaucer's; but the elaborate
"Orison to the Holy Virgin," beginning

> Mother of God, and Virgin undefiled,

seems to be correctly described as *Oratio Gallfridi
Chaucer ;* and in *Chaucer's A. B. C., called La Prière
de Notre Dame*, a translation by him from a French
original, we have a long address to the Blessed Virgin in
twenty-three stanzas, each of which begins with one of the
letters of the alphabet arranged in proper succession. Nor,
apart from this religious sentiment, had men yet altogether
lost sight of the ideal of true knightly love, destined
though this ideal was to be obscured in the course of
time, until at last the *Mort d'Arthure* was the favourite
literary nourishment of the minions and mistresses of
Edward IV.'s degenerate days. In his *Book of the Duchess*
Chaucer has left us a picture of true knightly love, together
with one of true maiden purity. The lady celebrated
in this poem was loth, merely for the sake of coquetting

with their exploits, to send her knights upon errands of
chivalry—

> into Walachy,
> To Prussia, and to Tartary,
> To Alexandria or Turkéy.

And doubtless there was many a gentle knight or squire
to whom might have been applied the description given
by the heroine of Chaucer's *Troilus and Cressid* of her
lover, and of that which attracted her in him :—

> For trust ye well that your estate royál,
> Nor vain delight, nor only worthiness
> Of you in war or tourney martial,
> Nor pomp, array, nobility, richés,
> Of these none made me rue on your distress ;
> *But moral virtue, grounded upon truth,*
> *That was the cause I first had on you ruth.*
>
> And gentle heart, and manhood that ye had,
> And that ye had (as méthought) in despite
> Everything that tended unto bad,
> As rudeness, and as popular appetite,
> And that your reason bridled your delight,
> 'Twas these did make 'bove every creatúre
> That I was yours, and shall while I may 'dure.

And if true affection under the law still secured the sympathy of the better-balanced part of society, so the vice of
those who made war upon female virtue, or the insolence
of those who falsely boasted of their conquests, still incurred its resentment. Among the companies which in
the *House of Fame* sought the favour of its mistress,
Chaucer vigorously satirises the would-be-lady-killers,
who were content with the *reputation* of accomplished
seducers ; and in *Troilus and Cressid* a shrewd observer
exclaims with the utmost vivacity against

> Such sort of folk,—what shall I clepe them ? what ?
> That vaunt themselves of women, and by name,
> That yet to them ne'er promised this or that,
> Nor knew them more, in sooth, than mine old hat.

The same easy but sagacious philosopher (Pandarus) observes, that the harm which is in this world springs as
often from folly as from malice. But a deeper feeling
animates the lament of the " good Alceste," in the Prologue to the *Legend of Good Women,* that among men the
betrayal of women is now " held a game." So indisputably it was already often esteemed, in too close an accordance with examples set in the highest places in the
land. If we are to credit an old tradition, a poem in which
Chaucer narrates the amours of Mars and Venus was written
by him at the request of John of Gaunt, to celebrate the
adultery of the duke's sister-in-law with a nobleman, to
whom the injured kinsman afterwards married one of his
own daughters ! But nowhere was the deterioration of sentiment on this head more strongly typified than in Edward
III. himself. The King, who (if the pleasing tale be true
which gave rise to some beautiful scenes in an old English
drama) had in his early days royally renounced an un-
lawful passion for the fair Countess of Salisbury, came to
be accused of at once violating his conjugal duty and
neglecting his military glory for the sake of strange
women's charms. The founder of the Order of the Garter
—the device of which enjoined purity even of thought as
a principle of conduct—died in the hands of a rapacious
courtesan. Thus, in England, as in France, the ascendancy is gained by ignobler views concerning the relation
between the sexes,—a relation to which the whole system
of chivalry owed a great part of its vitality, and on the
view of which prevailing in the most influential class of

any nation, the social health of that nation must inevitably in no small measure depend. Meanwhile, the
artificialities by means of which in France, up to the
beginning of the fifteenth century, it was sought to keep
alive an organised system of sentimentality in the social
dealings between gentlemen and ladies, likewise found
admission in England, but only in a modified degree.
Here the fashion in question asserted itself only, or
chiefly, in our poetic literature, and in the adoption by it
of such fancies as the praise and worship of the daisy, with
which we meet in the Prologue to Chaucer's *Legend of
Good Women*, and in the *Flower and the Leaf*, a most
pleasing poem (suggested by a French model), which .it
is unfortunately no longer possible to number among his
genuine works.   The poem of the *Court of Love*, which
was likewise long erroneously attributed to him, may be
the original work of an English author ; but in any case
its main contents are a mere adaptation of a peculiar
outgrowth on a foreign soil of conceptions common to
chivalry in general.

Of another force, which in the Middle Ages shared
with chivalry (though not with it alone) the empire over
the minds of men, it would certainly be rash to assert that
its day was passing away in the latter half of the fourteenth century.   It has indeed been pointed out that the
date at which Wyclif's career as a reformer may be
said to have begun almost coincides with that of the
climax and first decline of feudal chivalry in England.
But, without seeking to interpret coincidences, we
know that, though the influence of the Christian Church
and that of its Roman branch in particular, has asserted
and re-asserted itself in various ways and degrees in
various ages, yet in England, as elsewhere, the epoch

of its moral omnipotence had come to an end many
generations before the disruption of its external framework.
In the fourteenth century men had long ceased to look
for the mediation of the Church between an overbearing
Crown and a baronage and commonalty eager for the
maintenance of their rights or for the assertion of their
claims. On the other hand, the conflicts which still re-
curred between the temporal power and the Church had
as little reference as ever to spiritual concerns. Undoubtedly, the authority of the Church over the minds
of the people still depended in the main upon the spiritual influence she exercised over them; and the desire
for a reformation of the Church, which was already
making itself felt in a gradually widening sphere, was
by the great majority of those who cherished it held
perfectly compatible with a recognition of her authority.
The world, it has been well said, needed an enquiry ex-
tending over three centuries, in order to learn to walk
without the aid of the Church of Rome. Wyclif, who
sought to emancipate the human conscience from reli-
ance upon any earthly authority intermediate between the
soul and its Maker, reckoned without his generation ; and
few, except those with whom audacity took the place
of argument, followed him to the extreme results of his
speculations. The Great Schism rather stayed than pro-
moted the growth of an English feeling against Rome,
since it was now no longer necessary to acknowledge a
Pope who seemed the henchman of the arch-foe across
the narrow seas.

But although the progress of English sentiment towards the desire for liberation from Rome was to be
interrupted by a long and seemingly decisive reaction,
yet in the fourteenth as in the sixteenth century the

most active cause of the alienation of the people from the
Church was the conduct of the representatives of the
Church themselves. The Reformation has most appropriately retained in history a name at first unsuspiciously
applied to the removal of abuses in the ecclesiastical administration and in the life of the clergy. What aid
could be derived by those who really hungered for spiritual
food, or what strength could accrue to the thoughtless
faith of the light-hearted majority, from many of the most
common varieties of the English ecclesiastic of the later
Middle Ages? Apart from the Italian and other foreign
holders of English benefices, who left their flocks to be
tended by deputy, and to be shorn by an army of the
most offensive kind of tax-gatherers, the native clergy
included many species, but among them few which, to the
popular eye, seemed to embody a high ideal of religious
life. The times had by no means come to an end when
many of the higher clergy sought to vie with the lay lords
in warlike prowess. Perhaps the martial Bishop of Nor-
wich, who, after persecuting the heretics at home, had
commanded an army of crusaders in Flanders, levied on
behalf of Pope Urban VI. against the anti-Pope Clement
VII. and his adherents, was in the poet Gower's mind
when he complains that while

> the law is rulèd so,
> That clerks unto the war intend,
> I wot not how they should amend
> The woeful world in other things,
> And so make peace between the kings
> After the law of charity,
> Which is the duty properly
> Belonging unto the priesthóod.

A more general complaint, however, was that directing
itself against the extravagance and luxury of life in which

the dignified clergy indulged.   The cost of these un-
spiritual pleasures the great prelates had ample means for
defraying in the revenues of their sees ; while lesser digni-
taries had to be active in levying their dues or the fines
of their courts, lest everything should flow into the recep-
tacles of their superiors.   So in Chaucer's *Friar's Tale*
an unfriendly Regular says of an archdeacon,—

> For smallë tithes and for small offering
> He made the people piteously to sing.
> For ere the bishop caught them on his hook,
> They were down in the archëdeacon's book.

As a matter of course, the worthy who filled the office of
Summoner to the court of the archdeacon in question, had
a keen eye for the profitable improprieties subject to its
penalties, and was aided in his efforts by the professional
abettors of vice whom he kept "ready to his hand."   Nor
is it strange that the undisguised worldliness of many
members of the clerical profession should have reproduced
itself in other lay subordinates, even in the parish clerks,
at all times apt to copy their betters, though we would
fain hope such was not the case with the parish clerk,
"the jolly Absalom" of the *Miller's Tale*.   The love of
gold had corrupted the acknowledged chief guardians of in-
corruptible treasures, even though few may have avowed
this love as openly as the "idle" *Canon*, whose *Yeoman* had
so strange a tale to tell to the Canterbury pilgrims concerning his master's absorbing devotion to the problem of the
multiplication of gold.   To what a point the popular discontent with the vices of the higher secular clergy had
advanced in the last decennium of the century, may be seen
from the poem called the *Complaint of the Ploughman*—
a production pretending to be by the same hand which in
the *Vision* had dwelt on the sufferings of the people and

on the sinfulness of the ruling classes. Justly or unjustly,
the indictment was brought against the priests of being
the agents of every evil influence among the people, the
soldiers of an army of which the true head was not God,
but Belial.

In earlier days the Church had known how to compen-
sate the people for the secular clergy's neglect, or imperfect
performance, of its duties. But in no respect had the
ecclesiastical world more changed than in this. The
older monastic Orders had long since lost themselves in
unconcealed worldliness ; how, for instance, had the
Benedictines changed their character since the remote
times when their Order had been the principal agent in
revivifying the religion of the land ! Now, they were
taunted with their very name, as having been bestowed
upon them " by antiphrasis," i. e. by contraries. From
many of their monasteries, and from the inmates who
dwelt in these comfortable halls, had vanished even all
pretence of disguise. Chaucer's *Monk* paid no attention
to the rule of St. Benedict, and of his disciple St. Maur,

> Because that it was old and somewhat strait ;

and preferred to fall in with the notions of later times. He
was an " outrider, that loved venery," and whom his
tastes and capabilities would have well qualified for the
dignified post of abbot. He had "full many a dainty
horse" in his stable, and the swiftest of greyhounds to
boot ; and rode forth gaily, clad in superfine furs and a
hood elegantly fastened with a gold pin, and tied into a
love-knot at the "greater end," while the bridle of his
steed jingled as if its rider had been as good a knight as
any of them—this last, by the way, a mark of ostentation
against which Wyclif takes occasion specially to inveigh.

This Monk (and Chaucer must say that he was wise in his
generation) could not understand why he should study
books and unhinge his mind by the effort; life was not
worth having at the price ; and no one knew better to
what use to put the pleasing gift of existence.   Hence
mine host of the Tabard, a very competent critic, had
reason for the opinion which he communicated to the
Monk :—

> It is a noble pasture where thou go'st ;
> Thou art not like a penitent or ghost.

In the Orders of nuns, certain corresponding features were
becoming usual.   But little in the way of religious guidance
could fall to the lot of a sisterhood presided over by such
a *Prioress* as Chaucer's Madame Eglantine, whose mind—
possibly because her nunnery fulfilled the functions of a
finishing school for young ladies—was mainly devoted to
French and deportment, or by such a one as the historical
Lady Juliana Berners, of a rather later date, whose leisure
hours produced treatises on hunting and hawking, and
who would probably have on behalf of her own sex echoed
the *Monk's* contempt for the prejudice against the partici-
pation of the Religious in field-sports :—

> He gave not for that text a pullèd hen
> That saith, that hunters be no holy men.

On the other hand, neither did the Mendicant Orders,
instituted at a later date purposely to supply what the
older Orders, as well as the secular clergy, seemed to have
grown incapable of furnishing, any longer satisfy the reason
of their being.   In the fourteenth century the Dominicans
or Black Friars, who at London dwelt in such magnificence
that king and Parliament often preferred a sojourn with
them to abiding at Westminster, had in general grown

D

accustomed to concentrate their activity upon the spiritual
direction of the higher classes.   But though they counted
among them Englishmen of eminence (one of these was
Chaucer's friend, "the philosophical Strode"), they in
truth never played a more than secondary part in this
country, to whose soil the delicate machinery of the In-
quisition, of which they were by choice the managers, was
never congenial.   Of far greater importance for the population of England at large was the Order of the Franciscans
or (as they were here wont to call themselves or to be called)
Minorites or Grey Friars.   To them the poor had habitually looked for domestic ministrations, and for the inspir-
ing and consoling eloquence of the pulpit; and they had
carried their labours into the midst of the suffering
population, not afraid of association with that poverty
which they were by their vow themselves bound to espouse,
or of contact with the horrors of leprosy and the plague.
Departing from the short-sighted policy of their. illustrious founder, they had become a learned, as well as
a ministering and preaching Order; and it was precisely
from among them that, at Oxford and elsewhere, sprang a
succession of learned monks, whose names are inseparably
connected with some of the earliest English growths of philosophical speculation and scientific research.   Nor is it possible to doubt that in the middle of the thirteenth century
the monks of this Order at Oxford had exercised an appreciable influence upon the beginnings of a political struggle
of unequalled importance for the progress of our constitu-
tional life.   But in the Franciscans also the fourteenth
century witnessed a change, which may be described as a
gradual loss of the qualities for which they had been
honourably distinguished; and in England, as elsewhere,
the spirit of the words which Dante puts into the mouth

of St. Francis of Assisi was being verified by his degenerate children :—

> So soft is flesh of mortals, that on earth
> A good beginning doth no longer last
> Than while an oak may bring its fruit to birth.

Outwardly, indeed, the Grey Friars might still often seem what their predecessors had been, and might thus retain a powerful influence over the unthinking crowd, and to sheer worldlings appear as heretofore to represent a trouble-some *memento* of unexciting religious obligations; "Preach not," says Chaucer's *Host*,

> " as friars do in Lent,
> That they for our old sins may make us weep,
> Nor in such wise thy tale make us to sleep."

But in general men were beginning to suspect the motives as well as to deride the practices of the Friars, to accuse them of lying against St. Francis, and to desiderate for them an actual abode of fire, resembling that of which in their favourite religious shows they were wont to present the mimic semblance to the multitude. It was they who became in England as elsewhere the purveyors of charms and the organisers of pious frauds, while the learning for which their Order had been famous was withering away into the yellow leaf of scholasticism. The Friar in general became the common butt of literary satire ; and though the populace still remained true to its favourite guides, a reaction was taking place in favour of the secular as against the regular clergy in the sympathies of the higher classes, and in the spheres of society most open to intellectual influences. The monks and the London multitude were at one time united against John of Gaunt, but it was from the ranks of the secular clergy that Wyclif came

forth to challenge the ascendancy of Franciscan scholasticism in his university. Meanwhile the poet who in the
Poor Parson of the Town paints his ideal of a Christian
minister—simple, poor, and devoted to his holy work,—
has nothing but contempt for the friars at large, and for
the whole machinery worked by them, half effete, and
half spasmodic, and altogether sham. In King Arthur's
time, says that accurate and unprejudiced observer the
Wife of Bath, the land was filled with fairies—*now* it is
filled with friars as thick as motes in the beam of the sun.
Among them there is the *Pardoner,* *i. e.* seller of pardons
(indulgences)—with his "haughty" sermons, delivered "by
rote " to congregation after congregation in the self-same
words, and everywhere accompanied by the self-same tricks
of anecdotes and jokes,—with his Papal credentials, and
with the pardons he has brought from Rome " all hot,"—
and with precious relics to rejoice the hearts of the faithful,
and to fill his own pockets with the proceeds : to wit, a
pillowcase covered with the veil of Our Lady, and a piece
of the sail of the ship in which St. Peter went out fishing
on the Lake of Gennesareth. This worthy, who lays bare his
own motives with unparalleled cynical brutality, is manifestly drawn from the life ;—or the portrait could not have
been accepted which was presented alike by Chaucer, and
by his contemporary Langland, and (a century and a half
later) in the plagiarism of the orthodox Catholic John
Heywood. There, again, is the *Limitour,* a friar licensed
to beg, and to hear confession and grant absolution, within
the *limits* of a certain district. He is described by Chaucer
with so much humour, that one can hardly suspect much
exaggeration in the sketch. In him we have the truly
popular ecclesiastic who springs from the people, lives
among the people, and feels with the people. He is the

true friend of the poor, and being such, has, as one might
say, his finger in every pie : for " a fly and a friar will fall
in every dish and every business." His readily-proffered
arbitration settles the differences of the humbler classes
at the "love-days," a favourite popular practice noted
already in the *Vision* of Langland ; nor is he a niggard
of the mercies which he is privileged to dispense :—

> Full sweetly did he hear confessión,
> And pleasant was his absolutión.
> He was an easy man to give penánce,
> Whereso wist to have a good pittánce ;
> For unto a poor Order for to give,
> Is signë that a man is well y-shrive ;
> For if he gave, he durstë make a vaunt
> He wistë that a man was répentant.
> For many a man so hard is of his heart
> He can not weep although he sorely smart.
> Therefore instead of weeping and of prayers
> Men must give silver to the poorë Freres.

Already in the French *Roman de la Rose* the rivalry
between the Friars and the Parish Priests is the theme of
much satire, evidently unfavourable to the former and
favourable to the latter ; but in England, where Langland
likewise dwells upon the jealousy between them, it was
specially accentuated by the assaults of Wyclif upon
the Mendicant Orders. Wyclif's Simple Priests, who
at first ministered with the approval of the Bishops,
differed from the Mendicants, first by not being beggars,
and secondly by being poor. They might perhaps have
themselves ultimately played the part of a new Order
in England, had not Wyclif himself by rejecting the
cardinal dogma of the Church severed these followers
of his from its organism and brought about their suppression. The question as to Chaucer's own attitude towards

the Wycliffite movement will be more conveniently
touched upon below ; but the tone is unmistakable of the
references or allusions to Lollardry which he occasionally
introduces into the mouth of his *Host*, whose voice is
that *vox populi* which the upper and middle classes so
often arrogate to themselves.   Whatever those classes
might desire, it was not to have "cockle sown" by un-
authorised intruders "in the corn" of their ordinary
instruction.   Thus there is a tone of genuine attachment
to the "vested interest" principle, and of aversion from
all such interlopers as lay preachers and the like, in the
Host's exclamation, uttered after the *Reeve* has been (in
his own style) "sermoning" on the topic of old age :—

> What availeth all this wit ?
> What ? should we speak all day of Holy Writ ?
> The devil surely made a reeve to preach ;

for which he is as well suited as a cobbler would be for
turning mariner or physician !

Thus, then, in the England of Chaucer's days we find
the Church still in possession of vast temporal wealth
and of great power and privileges,—as well as of means for
enforcing unity of profession which the legislation of the
Lancastrian dynasty, stimulated by the prevailing fears of
heresy, was still further to increase.   On the other hand,
we find the influence of the clergy over the minds of the
people diminished though not extinguished.   This was,
in the case of the higher secular clergy, partly attributable
to their self-indulgence or neglect of their functions, partly
to their having been largely superseded by the Regulars
in the control of the religious life of the people.   The
Orders we find no longer at the height of their influence,
but still powerful by their wealth, their numbers, their

traditional hold upon the lower classes, and their determination to retain this hold even by habitually resorting to the most dubious of methods. Lastly, we find in the lower secular clergy, and doubtless may also assume it to have lingered among some of the regular, some of the salt left whose savour consists in a single-minded and humble resolution to maintain the highest standard of a religious life. But such " clerks " as these are at no times the most easily found, because it is not they who are always running " unto London, unto St. Paul's " on urgent private affairs. What wonder, that the real teaching of Wyclif, of which the full significance could hardly be understood, but by a select few, should have virtually fallen dead upon his generation, to which the various agitations and agitators, often mingling ideas of religious reform with social and political grievances, seemed to be identical in character and alike to require suppression! In truth, of course, these movements and their agents were often very different from one another in their ends, and were not to be suppressed by the same processes.

It should not be forgotten that in this century learning was, though only very gradually, ceasing to be a possession of the clergy alone. Much doubt remains as to the extent of education—if a little reading and less writing deserve the name—among the higher classes in this period of our national life. A cheering sign appears in the circumstance that the legal deeds of this age begin to bear signatures, and a reference to John of Trevisa would bear out Hallam's conjecture, that in the year 1400 "the average instruction of an English gentleman of the first class would comprehend common reading and writing, a considerable knowledge of French, and a slight tincture of Latin." Certain it is that in this century the barren teaching of

the Universities advanced but little towards the true end
of all academical teaching—the encouragement and spread
of the highest forms of national culture.   To what use
could a gentleman of Edward III.'s or Richard II.'s day
have put the acquirements of a *Clerk of Oxenford* in
Aristotelian logic, supplemented perhaps by a knowledge of
Priscian, and the rhetorical works of Cicero ?   Chaucer's
scholar, however much his learned modesty of manner and
sententious brevity of speech may commend him to our
sympathy and taste, is a man wholly out of the world in
which he lives, though a dependent on its charity even
for the means with which to purchase more of his beloved
books.   Probably no trustworthier conclusions as to
the literary learning and studies of those days are to be
derived from any other source than from a comparison
of the few catalogues of contemporary libraries remaining to us ; and these help to show that the century was
approaching its close before a few sparse rays of the
first dawn of the Italian Renascence reached England.
But this ray was communicated neither through the
clergy nor through the Universities ; and such influence
as was exercised by it upon the national mind, was
directly due to profane poets,—men of the world, who like
Chaucer quoted authorities even more abundantly than
they used them, and made some of their happiest dis-
coveries after the fashion in which the *Oxford Clerk*
came across Petrarch's Latin version of the story of
Patient Grissel : as it were by accident.   There is only
too ample a justification for leaving aside the records of
the history of learning in England during the latter half
of the fourteenth century in any sketch of the main influences which in that period determined or affected the
national progress.   It was not by his theological learning

that Wyclif was brought into living contact with the
current of popular thought and feeling. The Universities
were thriving exceedingly on the scholastic glories of
previous ages; but the ascendancy was passing away to
which Oxford had attained over Paris—during the earlier
middle ages, and again in the fifteenth century until the
advent of the Renascence, the central university of Europe
in the favourite study of scholastic philosophy and theology.

But we must turn from particular classes and ranks of
men to the whole body of the population, exclusively of
that great section of it which unhappily lay outside the
observation of any but a very few writers—whether poets or
historians. In the people at large we may, indeed, easily
discern in this period the signs of an advance towards
that self-government which is the true foundation of our
national greatness. But on the other hand it is impossible
not to observe how, while the moral ideas of the people
were still under the control of the Church, the State in
its turn still ubiquitously interfered in the settlement of
the conditions of social existence, fixing prices, controlling
personal expenditure, regulating wages. Not until England had fully attained to the character of a commercial
country, which it was coming gradually to assume, did
its inhabitants begin to understand the value of that
which has gradually come to distinguish ours among
the nations of Europe, viz. the right of individual Englishmen, as well as of the English people, to manage their
own affairs for themselves. This may help to explain
what can hardly fail to strike a reader of Chaucer and of
the few contemporary remains of our literature. About
our national life in this period, both in its virtues and in
its vices, there is something—it matters little whether we
call it—childlike or childish ; in its " apert " if not in

its "privy" sides it lacks the seriousness belonging to
men and to generations, who have learnt to control themselves, instead of relying on the control of others.

In illustration of this assertion, appeal might be made
to several of the most salient features in the social life of
the period. The extravagant expenditure in dress, fostered
by a love of pageantry of various kinds encouraged by
both chivalry and the Church, has been already referred
to ; it was by no means distinctive of any one class of
the population.   Among the friars who went about
preaching homilies on the people's favourite vices some
humorous rogues may, like the *Pardoner* of the *Canterbury Tales*, have made a point of treating their own
favourite vice as their one and unchangeable text :—

> My theme is always one, and ever was :
> *Radix malorum est cupiditas.*

But others preferred to dwell on specifically lay sins ; and
these moralists occasionally attributed to the love of expenditure on dress the impoverishment of the kingdom, forgetting in their ignorance of political economy and defiance
of common sense, that this result was really due to the
endless foreign wars.   Yet in contrast with the pomp
and ceremony of life, upon which so great an amount of
money and time and thought was wasted, are noticeable
shortcomings by no means uncommon in the case of
undeveloped civilisations (as for instance among the most
typically childish or childlike nationalities of the Europe
of our own day), viz. discomfort and uncleanliness of all
sorts.   To this may be added the excessive fondness for
sports and pastimes of all kinds, in which nations are
aptest to indulge before or after the era of their highest
efforts,—the desire to make life one long holiday, dividing

it between tournaments and the dalliance of courts of love,
or between archery-meetings (skilfully substituted by
royal command for less useful exercises), and the seductive
company of "tumblers," "fruiterers," and "waferers."
Furthermore, one may notice in all classes a far from eradi-
cated inclination to superstitions of every kind,—whether
those encouraged or those discouraged [1] by the Church,—
an inclination unfortunately fostered rather than checked
by the uncertain gropings of contemporary science. Hence,
the credulous acceptance of relics like those sold by the
Pardoner, and of legends like those related to Chaucer's
Pilgrims by the *Prioress* (one of the numerous repeti-
tions of a cruel calumny against the Jews), and by the
Second Nun (the supra-sensual story of Saint Cecilia).
Hence, on the other hand, the greedy hunger for the mar-
vels of astrology and alchemy, notwithstanding the growing scepticism even of members of a class represented
by Chaucer's *Franklin* towards

> such folly
> As in our days is not held worth a fly,

and notwithstanding the exposure of fraud by repentant or
sickened accomplices, such as the gold-making *Canon's
Yeoman*. Hence, again, the vitality of such quasi-scientific
fancies as the magic mirror, of which miraculous instrument
the *Squire's* " half-told story " describes a specimen, referring to the incontestable authority of Aristotle and others,
who write " in their lives " concerning quaint mirrors and
perspective glasses, as is well known to those who have
" heard the books " of these sages. Hence, finally, the cor-

---

[1] For holy Church's faith, in our belief,
Suffereth no illusion us to grieve.
The Franklin's Tale.

responding tendency to eschew the consideration of serious religious questions, and to leave them to clerks, as if they were crabbed problems of theology. For in truth, while the most fertile and fertilising ideas of the Middle Ages had exhausted, or were rapidly coming to exhaust, their influence upon the people, the forms of the doctrines of the Church—even of the most stimulative as well as of the most solemn among them,—had grown hard and stiff. To those who received if not to those who taught these doctrines they seemed alike lifeless, unless translated into the terms of the merest earthly transactions or the language of purely human relations. And thus, paradoxical as it might seem, cool-headed and conscientious rulers of the Church thought themselves on occasion called upon to restrain rather than to stimulate the religious ardour of the multitude—fed as the flame was by very various materials. Perhaps no more characteristic narrative has come down to us from the age of the poet of the *Canterbury Tales,* than the story of Bishop (afterwards Archbishop) Sudbury and the Canterbury Pilgrims. In the year 1370 the land was agitated through its length and breadth, on the occasion of the fourth jubilee of the national saint, Thomas the Martyr. The pilgrims were streaming in numbers along the familiar Kentish road, when, on the very vigil of the feast, one of their companies was accidentally met by the Bishop of London. They demanded his blessing ; but to their astonishment and indignation he seized the occasion to read a lesson to the crowd on the uselessness to unrepentant sinners of the plenary indulgences, for the sake of which they were wending their way to the Martyr's shrine. The rage of the multitude found a mouthpiece in a soldier, who loudly upbraided the Bishop for stirring up the people against

St. Thomas, and warned him that a shameful death would
befall him in consequence. The multitude shouted *Amen*
—and one is left to wonder whether any of the pious pilgrims who resented Bishop Sudbury's manly truthfulness,
swelled the mob which eleven years later butchered " the
plunderer," as it called him, "of the Commons." It is
such glimpses as this which show us how important the
Church had become towards the people. Worse was to
ensue before the better came ; in the meantime, the nation
was in that stage of its existence when the innocence of
the child was fast losing itself, without the self-control
of the man having yet taken its place.

But the heart of England was sound the while. The
national spirit of enterprise' was not dead in any class,
from knight to shipman ; and faithfulness and chastity in
woman were still esteemed the highest though not the
universal virtues of her sex. The value of such evidence
as the mind of a great poet speaking in his works furnishes for a knowledge of the times to which he belongs
is inestimable. For it shows us what has survived, as well
as what was doomed to decay, in the life of the nation
with which that mind was in sensitive sympathy. And
it therefore seemed not inappropriate to approach, in the
first instance, from this point of view the subject of this
biographical essay,—Chaucer, "the poet of the dawn."
For in him there are many things significant of the age
of transition in which he lived ; in him the mixture of
Frenchman and Englishman is still in a sense incomplete,
as that of their language is in the diction of his poems.
His gaiety of heart is hardly English ; nor is his willing
(though, to be sure, not invariably unquestioning) acceptance of forms into the inner meaning of which he does
not greatly vex his soul by entering ; nor his airy way of

ridiculing what he has no intention of helping to over-
throw; nor his light unconcern in the question whether
he is, or is not, an immoral writer.   Or, at least, in all
of these things he has no share in qualities and tendencies,
which influences and conflicts unknown to and unforeseen
by him may be safely said to have ultimately made
characteristic of Englishmen.   But he *is* English in his
freedom and frankness of spirit; in his manliness of mind;
in his preference for the good in things as they are to the
good in things as they might be; in his loyalty, his piety,
his truthfulness.   Of the great movement which was to
mould the national character for at least a long series of
generations he displays no serious foreknowledge; and of
the elements already preparing to affect the course of that
movement he shows a very incomplete consciousness.   But
of the health and strength which, after struggles many and
various, made that movement possible and made it victo-
rious, he, more than any one of his contemporaries, is the
living type and the speaking witness.   Thus, like the
times to which he belongs, he stands half in and half out
of the Middle Ages, half in and half out of a phase of our
national life, which we can never hope to understand more
than partially and imperfectly.   And it is this, taken together with the fact that he is the first English poet to
read whom is to enjoy him, and that he garnished not only
our language but our literature with blossoms still adorn-
ing them in vernal freshness,—which makes Chaucer's
figure so unique a one in the gallery of our great English
writers, and gives to his works an interest so inexhaustible
for the historical as well as for the literary student.

CHAPTER II.

CHAUCER'S LIFE AND WORKS.

SOMETHING has been already said as to the conflict of
opinion concerning the period of Geoffrey Chaucer's birth,
the precise date of which is very unlikely ever to be ascer-
tained. A better fortune has attended the anxious enquiries which in his case, as in those of other great men
have been directed to the very secondary question of
ancestry and descent,—a question to which, in the abstract
at all events, no man ever attached less importance than
he. Although the name *Chaucer* is (according to Thynne),
to be found on the lists of Battle Abbey, this no more
proves that the poet himself came of "high parage," than
the reverse is to be concluded from the nature of his coat-
of-arms, which Speght thought must have been taken out
of the 27th and 28th Propositions of the First Book of
Euclid. Many a warrior of the Norman Conquest was
known to his comrades only by the name of the trade
which he had plied in some French or Flemish town,
before he attached himself a volunteer to Duke William's
holy and lucrative expedition ; and it is doubtful whether
even in the fourteenth century the name *Le Chaucer* is,
wherever it occurs in London, used as a surname, or
whether in some instances it is not merely a designation
of the owner's trade. Thus we should not be justified in

assuming a French origin for the family from which Richard le Chaucer, whom we know to have been the poet's grandfather, was descended. Whether or not he was at any time a shoemaker (*chaucier*, maker of *chausses*), and accordingly belonged to a gentle craft otherwise not unassociated with the history of poetry, Richard was a citizen of London, and vintner, like his son John after him. John Chaucer, whose wife's Christian name may be with tolerable safety set down as Agnes, owned a house in Thames Street, London, not far from the arch on which modern pilgrims pass by rail to Canterbury or beyond, and in the neighbourhood of the great bridge, which in Chaucer's own day, emptied its travellers on their errands, sacred or profane, into the great Southern road, the *Via Appia* of England. The house afterwards descended to John's son, GEOFFREY, who released his right to it by deed in the year 1380. Chaucer's father was probably a man of some substance, the most usual personal recommendation to great people in one of his class. For he was at least temporarily connected with the Court, inasmuch as he attended King Edward III. and Queen Philippa on the memorable journey to Flanders and Germany, in the course of which the English monarch was proclaimed Vicar of the Holy Roman Empire on the left bank of the Rhine. John Chaucer died in 1366, and in course of time his widow married another citizen and vintner. Thomas Heyroun, John Chaucer's brother of the half-blood, was likewise a member of the same trade ; so that the young Geoffrey was certainly not brought up in an atmosphere of abstinence. The *Host* of the *Canterbury Tales*, though he takes his name from an actual personage, may therefore have in him touches of a family portrait ; but Chaucer himself nowhere displays any traces

of a hereditary devotion to Bacchus, and makes so experienced a practitioner as the *Pardoner* the mouthpiece
of as witty an invective against drunkenness as has been
uttered by any assailant of our existing licensing laws.
Chaucer's own practice as well as his opinion on this head
is sufficiently expressed in the characteristic words he
puts into the mouth of Cressid :—

> In every thing, I wot, there lies measúre :
> For though a man forbid all drunkenness,
> He biddeth not that every créature
> Be drinkless altogether, as I guess.

Of Geoffrey Chaucer we know nothing whatever from
the day of his birth (whenever it befell) to the year 1357.
His earlier biographers, who supposed him to have been
born in 1328, had accordingly a fair field open for conjecture and speculation.   Here it must suffice to risk the
asseveration, that he cannot have accompanied his father
to Cologne in 1338, and on that occasion have been first
"taken notice of" by king and queen, if he was not
born till two or more years afterwards.   If, on the other
hand, he was born in 1328, both events *may* have taken
place.   On neither supposition is there any reason for
believing that he studied at one—or at both—of our
English Universities.   The poem cannot be accepted as
Chaucerian, the author of which (very possibly by a
mere dramatic assumption) declares :—

> Philogenet I call'd am far and near,
> Of Cambridge clerk;

nor can any weight be attached to the circumstance that
the *Clerk*, who is one of the most delightful figures among
the Canterbury Pilgrims, is an Oxonian.   The enticing
enquiry as to *which* of the sister Universities may claim

E

Chaucer as her own must, therefore, be allowed to drop, together with the subsidiary question, whether stronger evidence of local colouring is furnished by the *Miller's* picture of the life of a poor scholar in lodgings at Oxford, or by the *Reeve's* rival narrative of the results of a Trumpington walk taken by two undergraduates of the "Soler Hall" at Cambridge. Equally baseless is the supposition of one of Chaucer's earliest biographers, that he completed his academical studies at Paris—and equally futile the concomitant fiction that in France "he acquired much applause by his literary exercises." Finally, we have the tradition that he was a member of the Inner Temple—which is a conclusion deduced from a piece of genial scandal as to a record having been seen in that Inn of a fine imposed upon him for beating a friar in Fleet-street. This story was early placed by Thynne on the horns of a sufficiently decisive dilemma : in the days of Chaucer's youth, lawyers had not yet been admitted into the Temple; and in the days of his maturity he is not very likely to have been found engaged in battery in a London thoroughfare.

We now desert the region of groundless conjecture, in order with the year 1357 to arrive at a firm though not very broad footing of facts. In this year, "Geoffrey Chaucer" (whom it would be too great an effort of scepticism to suppose to have been merely a namesake of the poet) is mentioned in the Household Book of Elizabeth Countess of Ulster, wife of Prince Lionel (third son of King Edward III., and afterwards Duke of Clarence), as a re-cipient of certain articles of apparel. Two similar notices of his name occur up to the year 1359. He is hence concluded to have belonged to Prince Lionel's establish-ment as squire or page to the Lady Elizabeth ; and it was

probably in the Prince's retinue that he took part in the
expedition of King Edward III. into France, which
began at the close of the year 1359 with the ineffectual
siege of Rheims, and in the next year, after a futile
attempt upon Paris, ended with the compromise of the
Peace of Brétigny. In the course of this campaign
Chaucer was taken prisoner; but he was released without
much loss of time, as appears by a document bearing date
March 1st, 1360, in which the king contributes the sum
of 16l. for Chaucer's ransom. We may therefore conclude that he missed the march upon Paris, and the
sufferings undergone by the English army on their road
thence to Chartres—the most exciting experiences of an
inglorious campaign; and that he was actually set free by
the Peace. When, in the year 1367, we next meet with
his name in authentic records, his earliest known patron,
the Lady Elizabeth, is dead; and he has passed out of
the service of Prince Lionel into that of King Edward
himself, as Valet of whose Chamber or household he
receives a yearly salary for life of twenty marks, for his
former and future services. Very possibly he had quitted
Prince Lionel's service when in 1361 that Prince had by
reason of his marriage with the heiress of Ulster been
appointed to the Irish government by his father, who was
supposed at one time to have destined him for the Scottish
throne.

Concerning the doings of Chaucer in the interval
between his liberation from his French captivity and the
first notice of him as Valet of the King's Chamber we
know nothing at all. During these years, however, no
less important a personal event than his marriage was by
earlier biographers supposed to have occurred. On the
other hand, according to the view which commends itself

to several eminent living commentators of the poet, it was
not courtship and marriage, but a hopeless and unrequited
passion, which absorbed these years of his life. Certain
stanzas in which, as they think, he gave utterance to this
passion are by them ascribed to one of these years; so that
if their view were correct, the poem in question would
have to be regarded as the earliest of his extant productions. The problem which we have indicated must
detain us for a moment.

It is attested by documentary evidence, that in the year
1374, Chaucer had a wife by name Philippa, who had been
in the service of John of Gaunt, Duke of Lancaster, and
of his Duchess (doubtless his second wife, Constance), as
well as in that of his mother the good Queen Philippa,
and who, on several occasions afterwards, besides special
new year's gifts of silver-gilt cups from the Duke, received
her annual pension of ten marks through her husband. It
is likewise proved that, in 1366, a pension of ten marks
was granted to *a* Philippa Chaucer, one of the ladies of
the Queen's Chamber. Obviously, it is a highly probable
assumption that these two Philippa Chaucers were one
and the same person; but in the absence of any direct proof
it is impossible to affirm as certain, or to deny as de-
monstrably untrue, that the Philippa Chaucer of 1366
owed her surname to marriage. Yet the view was long
held, and is still maintained by writers of knowledge
and insight, that the Philippa of 1366 was at that date
Chaucer's wife. In or before that year he married, it was
said, Philippa Roet, daughter of Sir Paon de Roet of
Hainault, Guienne King of Arms, who came to England in
Queen Philippa's retinue in 1328. This tradition derived
special significance from the fact that another daughter of
Sir Paon, Katharine, widow of Sir Hugh Swynford, was

successively governess, mistress, and (third) wife to the
Duke of Lancaster, to whose service both Geoffrey and
Philippa Chaucer were at one time attached. It was
apparently founded on the circumstance that Thomas
Chaucer, the supposed son of the poet, quartered the Roet
arms with his own. But unfortunately there is no evidence
to show that Thomas Chaucer was a son of Geoffrey ; and
the superstructure must needs vanish with its basis. It
being then no longer indispensable to assume Chaucer to
have been a married man in 1366, the Philippa Chaucer
of that year *may* have been only a namesake, and possibly
a relative, of Geoffrey ; for there were other Chaucers in
London besides him and his father (who died this year),
and one Chaucer at least has been found who was well-to-do
enough to have a Damsel of the Queen's Chamber for his
daughter in these certainly not very exclusive times.

There is accordingly no *proof* that Chaucer was a married
man before 1374, when he is known to have received a
pension for his own and his wife's services. But with
this negative result we are asked not to be poor-spirited
enough to rest content. At the opening of his *Book of
the Duchess,* a poem certainly written towards the end of
the year 1369, Chaucer makes use of certain expressions,
both very pathetic and very definite. The most obvious
interpretation of the lines in question seems to be that they
contain the confession of a hopeless passion, which has
lasted for eight years—a confession which certainly seems
to come more appropriately and more naturally from an
unmarried than from a married man. " For eight years,"
he says, or seems to say, " I have loved, and loved in vain
—and yet my cure is never the nearer. There is but one
physician that can heal me—but all that is ended and
done with. Let us pass on into fresh fields ; what cannot

be obtained must needs be left." It seems impossible to
interpret this passage (too long to cite *in extenso*) as a
complaint of married life.   Many other poets have indeed
complained of their married lives, and Chaucer (if the
view to be advanced below be correct) as emphatically as any.
But though such occasional exclamations of impatience or
regret—more especially when in a comic vein—may receive
pardon, or even provoke amusement, yet a serious and
sustained poetic version of Sterne's " *sum multum fatigatus
de uxore mea* " would be unbearable in any writer of self-
respect, and wholly out of character in Chaucer.   Even
Byron only indited elegies about his married life after his
wife *had left him.*

Now, among Chaucer's minor poems is preserved one
called the *Complaint of the Death of Pity,* which purports
to set forth " how pity is dead and buried in a gentle
heart," and, after testifying to a hopeless passion, ends with
the following declaration, addressed to Pity, as in a " bill"
or letter :—

> This is to say : I will be yours for ever,
> Though ye me slay by Cruelty, your foe ;
> Yet shall my spirit nevermore dissever
> From your service, for any pain or woe,
> Pity, whom I have sought so long ago !
> Thus for your death I may well weep and plain,
> With heart all sore, and full of busy pain.

If this poem be autobiographical, it would indisputably
correspond well enough to a period in Chaucer's life, and
to a mood of mind preceding those to which the introduction to the *Book of the Duchess* belongs.   If it be not
autobiographical—and in truth there is nothing to prove
it such, so that an attempt has been actually made to
suggest its having been intended to apply to the expe-

riences of another man—then the *Complaint of Pity* has no special value for students of Chaucer, since its poetic beauty, as there can be no harm in observing, is not in itself very great.

To come to an end of this topic, there seems no possibility of escaping from one of the following alternatives. *Either* the Philippa Chaucer of 1366 was Geoffrey Chaucer's wife, whether or not she was Philippa Roet before marriage, and the lament of 1369 had reference to another lady—anassumption to be regretted in the case of a married man, but not out of the range of possibility. *Or*—and this seems on the whole the most probable view —the Philippa Chaucer of 1366 was a namesake whom Geoffrey married some time after 1369, possibly, (of course only *possibly,*) the very lady whom he had loved hopelessly for eight years, and persuaded himself that he had at last relinquished—and who had then relented after all. This last conjecture it is certainly difficult to reconcile with the conclusion at which we arrive on other grounds, that Chaucer's married life was not one of preponderating bliss. That he and his wife were *cousins* is a pleasing thought, but one which is not made more pleasing by the seeming fact that, if they were so related, marriage in their case failed to draw close that hearts' bond which such kinship at times half unconsciously knits.

Married or still a bachelor, Chaucer may fairly be supposed, during part of the years previous to that in which we find him securely established in the king's service, to have enjoyed a measure of independence and leisure open to few men in his rank of life, when once the golden days of youth and early manhood have passed away. Such years are in many men's lives marked by the projection, or even by the partial accomplishment, of literary

undertakings on a large scale, and more especially of
such as partake of an imitative character. When
a juvenile and facile writer's taste is still unsettled, and
his own style is as yet unformed, he eagerly tries his hand
at the reproduction of the work of others; translates the
Iliad or *Faust*, or suits himself with unsuspecting prompti-
tude to the production of masques, or pastorals, or life
dramas—or whatever may be the prevailing fashion in
poetry—after the manner of the favourite literary models
of the day. *A priori*, therefore, everything is in favour
of the belief hitherto universally entertained, that among
Chaucer's earliest poetical productions was the extant
English translation of the French *Roman de la Rose*. That
he made *some* translation of this poem is a fact resting on
his own statement in a passage indisputably written by
him (in the *Prologue* to the *Legend of Good Women*); nor
is the value of this statement reduced by the negative
circumstance, that in the extraordinary tag (if it may be
called by so irreverent a name) to the extant *Canterbury
Tales*, the *Romaunt of the Rose* is passed over in silence,
or at least not nominally mentioned, among the objectionable works which the poet is there made to retract. And
there seems at least no necessity for giving in to the conclusion that Chaucer's translation has been lost, and was
not that which has been hitherto accepted as his. For
this conclusion is based upon the use of a formal test,
which in truth need not be regarded as of itself absolutely
decisive in any case, but which in this particular instance
need not be held applicable at all. A particular rule
against rhyming with one another particular sounds,
which in his later poems Chaucer seems invariably to have
followed, need not have been observed by him in what
was actually, or all but, his earliest. The unfinished state

of the extant translation accords with the supposition that
Chaucer broke it off on adopting (possibly after conference
with Gower, who likewise observes the rule) a more logical
practice as to the point in question. Moreover, no English
translation of this poem besides Chaucer's is ever known
to have existed.

Whither should the youthful poet, when in search of
materials on which to exercise a ready but as yet untrained
hand, have so naturally turned as to French poetry, and
in its domain whither so eagerly as to its universally
acknowledged master-piece ? French verse was the delight
of the Court, into the service of which he was about this
time preparing permanently to enter, and with which he
had been more or less connected from his boyhood. In
French Chaucer's contemporary Gower composed not only
his first longer work, but not less than fifty ballads or
sonnets, and in French (as well as in English) Chaucer
himself may have possibly in his youth set his own
'prentice hand to the turning of " *ballades, rondels, vire-
layes.*" The time had not yet arrived, though it was not
far distant, when his English verse was to attest his admiration of Machault, whose fame Froissart and Froissart's
imitations had brought across from the French Court to the
English ; and when Gransson, who served King Richard II.
as a squire, was extolled by his English adapter as the
" flower of them that write in France." But as yet Chaucer's
own tastes, his French blood, if he had any in his veins,
and the familiarity with the French tongue which he had
already had opportunities of acquiring, were more likely
to commend to him productions of broader literary merits
and a wider popularity. From these points of view, in
the days of Chaucer's youth, there was no rival to the
Roman de la Rose, one of those rare works on which the

literary history of whole generations and centuries may be said to hinge. The Middle Ages, in which from various causes the literary intercommunication between the nations of Europe was in some respects far livelier than it has been in later times, witnessed the appearance of several such works—diverse in kind but similar to one another in the universality of their popularity: the *Consolation of Philosophy*, the *Divine Comedy*, the *Imitation of Christ*, the *Roman de la Rose*, the *Ship of Fools*. The favour enjoyed by the *Roman de la Rose*, was in some ways the most extraordinary of all. In France, this work remained the dominant work of poetic literature, and " the source whence every rhymer drew for his needs " down to the period of the classical revival led by Ronsard (when it was edited by Clement Marot, Spenser's early model). In England, it exercised an influence only inferior to that which belonged to it at home upon both the matter and the form of poetry down to the renascence begun by Surrey and Wyatt. This extraordinary literary influence admits of a double explanation. But just as the authorship of the poem was very unequally divided between two personages, wholly divergent in their purposes as writers, so the *popularity* of the poem is probably in the main to be attributed to the second and later of the pair.

To the *trouvère* Guillaume de Lorris (who took his name from a small town in the valley of the Loire) was due the original conception of the *Roman de la Rose*, for which it is needless to suspect any extraneous source. To novelty of subject he added great ingenuity of treatment. Instead of a narrative of warlike adventures he offered to his readers a psychological romance, in which a combination of symbolisations and personified abstractions supplied the characters of the moral conflict represented.

Bestiaries and Lapidaries had familiarised men's minds with the art of finding a symbolical significance in particular animals and stones ; and the language of poets was becoming a language of flowers. On the other hand, the personification of abstract qualities was a usage largely affected by the Latin writers of the earlier Middle Ages, and formed a favourite device of the monastic beginnings of the Christian drama. For both these literary fashions, which mildly exercised the ingenuity while deeply gratifying the tastes of mediæval readers, room was easily found by Guillaume de Lorris within a framework in itself both appropriate and graceful. He told (as reproduced by his English translator) how in a dream he seemed to himself to wake up on a May morning. Sauntering forth, he came to a garden surrounded by a wall, on which were depicted many unkindly figures, such as Hate and Villainy, and Avarice and Old Age, and another thing

> That seemèd like a hypocrite,
> And it was clepèd pope holy.

Within, all seemed so delicious that, feeling ready to give an hundred pound for the chance of entering, he smote at a small wicket and was admitted by a courteous maiden named Idleness. On the sward in the garden were dancing its owner, Sir Mirth, and a company of friends ; and by the side of Gladness the dreamer saw the God of Love and his attendant, a bachelor named Sweet-looking, who bore two bows, each with five arrows. Of these bows the one was straight and fair, and the other crooked and unsightly, and each of the arrows bore the name of some quality or emotion by which love is advanced or hindered. And as the dreamer was gazing into the spring

of Narcissus (the imagination), he beheld a rose-tree
" charged full of roses," and, becoming enamoured of
one of them, eagerly advanced to pluck the object of his
passion.   In the midst of this attempt he was struck by
arrow upon arrow, shot " wonder smart " by Love from
the strong bow.   The arrow called Company completes
the victory; the dreaming poet becomes the Lover
(*L'Amant*), and swears allegiance to the God of Love, who
proceeds to instruct him in his laws ; and the real action
(if it is to be called such) of the poem begins.   This consists in the Lover's desire to possess himself of the Rose-
bud, the opposition offered to him by powers both good
and evil, and by Reason in particular, and the support
which he receives from more or less discursive friends.
Clearly, the conduct of such a scheme as this admits of
being varied in many ways and protracted to any length ;
but its first conception is easy and natural, and when it
was novel to boot, was neither commonplace nor ill-
chosen.

After writing about one-fifth of the 22,000 verses of
which the original French poem consists, Guillaume de
Lorris, who had executed his part of the task in full sympathy with the spirit of the chivalry of his times, died,
and left the work to be continued by another *trouvère*,
Jean de Meung (so-called from the town, near Lorris, in
which he lived).   " Hobbling John " took up the thread
of his predecessor's poem in the spirit of a wit and an
encyclopædist.   Indeed, the latter appellation suits him
in both its special and its general sense.   Beginning with
a long dialogue between Reason and the Lover, he was
equally anxious to display his freedom of criticism and his
universality of knowledge, both scientific and anecdotical.
His vein was pre-eminently satirical and abundantly allu-

sive; and among the chief objects of his satire are the two favourite themes of mediæval satire in general, religious hypocrisy (personified in *Faux-Semblant*, who has been described as one of the ancestors of *Tartuffe*), and the foibles of women. To the gross salt of Jean de Meung, even more than to the courtly perfume of Guillaume de Lorris, may be ascribed the long-lived popularity of the *Roman de la Rose;* and thus a work, of which already the theme and first conception imply a great step forwards from the previous range of mediæval poetry, became a favourite with all classes by reason of the piquancy of its flavour, and the quotable applicability of many of its passages. Out of a chivalrous allegory Jean de Meung had made a popular satire; and though in its completed form it could look for no welcome in many a court or castle,—though Petrarch despised it, and Gerson in the name of the Church recorded a protest against it,—and though a bevy of offended ladies had well-nigh taken the law into their own hands against its author,—yet it commanded a vast public of admirers. And against such a popularity even an offended clergy, though aided by the sneers of the fastidious and the vehemence of the fair, is wont to contend in vain.

Chaucer's translation of this poem is thought to have been the cause which called forth from Eustace Deschamps, Machault's pupil and nephew, the complimentary *ballade* in the refrain of which the Englishman is saluted as

Grant translateur, noble Geffroi Chaucier.

But whether or not such was the case, his version of the *Roman de la Rose* seems, on the whole, to be a translation properly so called—although, considering the great num-

ber of MSS. existing of the French original, it would
probably be no easy task to verify the assertion that in
one or the other of these are to be found the few passages
thought to have been interpolated by Chaucer. On the
other hand, his omissions are extensive ; indeed, the
whole of his translation amounts to little more than
one-third of the French original. It is all the more noteworthy that Chaucer reproduces only about one-half of the
part contributed by Jean de Meung, and again condenses
this half to one-third of its length. In general, he has
preserved the French names of localities, and even occasionally helps himself to a rhyme by retaining a French
word. Occasionally he shows a certain timidity as a translator, speaking of " the tree which in France men call a
pine," and pointing out, so that there may be no mistake,
that mermaidens are called " sereyns " (*sirènes*) in France.
On the other hand, his natural vivacity now and then
suggests to him a turn of phrase or an illustration of his
own. As a loyal English courtier he cannot compare a fair
bachelor to any one so aptly as to " the lord's son of
Windsor ;" and as writing not far from the time when
the Statute of Kilkenny was passed, he cannot lose the
opportunity of inventing an Irish parentage for Wicked-
Tongue :

> So full of cursèd rage
> It well agreed with his lineáge ;
> For him an Irishwoman bare.

The debt which Chaucer in his later works owed to the
Roman of the Rose was considerable, and by no means
confined to the favourite May-morning exordium and
the recurring machinery of a vision—to the origin of
which latter (the dream of Scipio related by Cicero and

expounded in the widely-read Commentary of Macrobius)
the opening lines of the *Romaunt* point.   He owes to the
French poem both the germs of felicitous phrases, such as
the famous designation of Nature as " the Vicar of the
Almighty Lord," and perhaps touches used by him in
passages like that in which he afterwards, with further
aid from other sources, drew the character of a true
gentleman.   But the main service which the work of this
translation rendered to him was the opportunity which it
offered of practising and perfecting a ready and happy
choice of words,—a service in which, perhaps, lies the
chief use of all translation, considered as an exercise of style.
How far he had already advanced in this respect, and how
lightly our language was already moulding itself in his
hands, may be seen from several passages in the poem ;
for instance, from that about the middle, where the old
and new theme of self-contradictoriness of love is treated
in endless variations.   In short, Chaucer executed his
task with facility, and frequently with grace, though for
one reason or another he grew tired of it before he had
carried it out with completeness.   Yet the translation (and
this may have been among the causes why he seems to
have wearied of it) has notwithstanding a certain air of
schoolwork ; and though Chaucer's next poem, to which
incontestable evidence assigns the date of the year 1369,
is still very far from being wholly original, yet the step is
great from the *Romaunt of the Rose* to the *Book of the
Duchess.*

Among the passages of the French *Roman de la Rose*
omitted in Chaucer's translation are some containing
critical reflexions on the character of kings and constituted authorities—a species of observations which kings
and constituted authorities have never been notorious for

loving. This circumstance, together with the reference to
Windsor quoted above, suggests the probability that
Chaucer's connexion with the Court had not been interrupted, or had been renewed, or was on the eve of renew-
ing itself, at the time when he wrote this translation. In
becoming a courtier, he was certainly placed within the
reach of social opportunities such as in his day he could
nowhere else have enjoyed. In England as well as in Italy
during the fourteenth and the two following centuries, as
the frequent recurrence of the notion attests, the "good"
courtier seemed the perfection of the idea of gentleman.
At the same time exaggerated conceptions of the courtly
breeding of Chaucer's and Froissart's age may very easily
be formed; and it is almost amusing to contrast with
Chaucer's generally liberal notions of manners, severe
views of etiquette like that introduced by him at the close
of the *Man of Law's Tale*, where he stigmatizes as a
solecism the statement of the author from whom he copied
his narrative, that King Ælla sent his little boy to invite
the emperor to dinner. "It is best to deem he went
himself."

The position which in June, 1367, we find Chaucer
holding at Court is that of "Valettus" to the King, or,
as a later document of May, 1368, has it, of "Valettus
Cameræ Regis"—Valet or Yeoman of the King's Chamber.
Posts of this kind, which involved the ordinary functions
of personal attendance—the making of beds, the holding
of torches, the laying of tables, the going on messages, &c.
—were usually bestowed upon young men of good family.
In due course of time a royal valet usually rose to the
higher post of royal squire—either "of the household"
generally, or of a more special kind. Chaucer appears in
1368 as an "esquire of less degree," his name standing

seventeenth in a list of seven-and-thirty. After the year 1373 he is never mentioned by the lower, but several times by Latin equivalents of the higher, title. Frequent entries occur of the pension or salary of twenty marks granted to him for life; and, as will be seen, he soon began to be employed on missions abroad. He had thus become a regular member of the royal establishment, within the sphere of which we must suppose the associations of the next years of his life to have been confined. They belonged to a period of peculiar significance both for the English people and for the Plantagenet dynasty, whose glittering exploits reflected so much transitory glory on the national arms. At home, these years were the brief interval between two of the chief visitations of the Black Death (1361 and 1369), and a few years earlier the poet of the *Vision* had given voice to the sufferings of the poor. It was not, however, the mothers of the people crying for their children whom the courtly singer remembered in his elegy written in the year 1369; the woe to which he gave a poetic expression was that of a princely widower temporarily inconsolable for the loss of his first wife. In 1367 the Black Prince was conquering Castile (to be lost again before the year was out) for that interesting protégé of the Plantagenets and representative of legitimate right, Don Pedro the Cruel, whose daughter the inconsolable widower was to espouse in 1372, and whose "tragic" downfall Chaucer afterwards duly lamented in his *Monk's Tale*:—

> O noble, O worthy Pedro, glory of Spain,
> Whom fortune held so high in majesty!

As yet the star of the valiant Prince of Wales had not been quenched in the sickness which was the harbinger of

F

death; and his younger brother, John of Gaunt, though
already known for his bravery in the field (he commanded
the reinforcements sent to Spain in 1367), had scarcely
begun to play the prominent part in politics which he
was afterwards to fill. But his day was at hand, and the
anti-clerical tenour of the legislation and of the administra-
tive changes of these years was in entire harmony with
the policy of which he was to constitute himself the
representative. 1365 is the year of the Statute of
Provisors, and 1371 that of the dismissal of William of
Wykeham.

John of Gaunt was born in 1340, and was, therefore,
probably of much the same age as Chaucer, and like him
now in the prime of life. Nothing could accordingly be
more natural than that a more or less ·intimate relation
should have formed itself between them. This relation,
there is reason to believe, afterwards ripened on Chaucer's
part into one of distinct political partisanship, of which
there could as yet (for the reason given above) hardly be
a question. There was, however, so far as we know,
nothing in Chaucer's tastes and tendencies to render it
antecedently unlikely that he should have been ready to
follow the fortunes of a prince who entered the political
arena as an adversary of clerical predominance. Had
Chaucer been a friend of it in principle, he would hardly
have devoted his first efforts as a writer to the translation
of the *Roman de la Rose*. In so far, therefore, and in
truth it is not very far, as John of Gaunt may be afterwards said to have been a Wycliffite, the same description
might probably be applied to Chaucer. With such sentiments a personal orthodoxy was fully reconcileable in both
patron and follower; and the so-called *Chaucer's A. B. C.*,
a version of a prayer to the Virgin in a French poetical

" Pilgrimage," might with equal probability have been put
together by him either early or late in the course of his life.
There was, however, a tradition, repeated by Speght, that
this piece was composed "at the request of Blanche,
Duchess of Lancaster, as a prayer for her private use, being
a woman in her religion very devout." If so, it must have
been written before the Duchess's death, which occurred
in 1369; and we may imagine it, if we please, with its
twenty-three initial letters blazoned in red and blue and
gold on a flyleaf inserted in the Book of the pious
Duchess,—herself, in the fervent language of the poem,
an illuminated calendar, as being lighted in this world
with the Virgin's holy name.

In the autumn of 1369, then, the Duchess Blanche
died an early death; and it is pleasing to know that John
of Gaunt, to whom his marriage with her had brought
wealth and a dukedom, ordered services, in pious remembrance of her, to be held at her grave.   The elaborate
elegy which—very possibly at the widowed Duke's
request—was composed by Chaucer, leaves no doubt as
to the identity of the lady whose loss it deplores :—

> —— goode faire *White* she hight;
> Thus was my lady named right;
> For she was both fair and bright.

But, in accordance with the taste of his age, which
shunned such sheer straightforwardness in poetry, the
Book of the Duchess contains no further transparent reference to the actual circumstances of the wedded life which
had come to so premature an end—for John of Gaunt
had married Blanche of Lancaster in 1359 ;—and an
elaborate framework is constructed round the essential
theme of the poem.   Already, however, the instinct of

Chaucer's own poetic genius had taught him the value of personal directness ; and, artificially as the course of the poem is arranged, it begins in the most artless and effective fashion with an account given by the poet of his own sleep- lessness and its cause already referred to—an opening so felicitous that it was afterwards imitated by Froissart. And so, Chaucer continues, as he could not sleep, to drive the night away he sat upright in his bed reading a "romance," which he thought better entertainment than chess or draughts.   The book which he read was the *Meta- morphoses* of Ovid ; and in it he chanced on the tale of Ceyx and Alcyone—the lovers whom, on their premature death, the compassion of Juno changed into the sea- birds that bring good luck to mariners.   Of this story (whether Chaucer derived it direct from Ovid, or from Machault's French version is disputed), the earlier part serves as the introduction to the poem.   The story breaks off—with the dramatic abruptness in which Chaucer is a master, and which so often distinguishes his versions from their originals—at the death of Alcyone, caused by her grief at the tidings brought by Morpheus of her husband's death.   Thus subtly the god of sleep and the death of a loving wife mingle their images in the poet's mind ; and with these upon him he falls asleep " right upon his book."

What more natural, after this, than the dream which came to him ?   It was May, and he lay in his bed at morning-time, having been awakened out of his slumbers by the "small fowls," who were carolling forth their notes— " some high, some low, and all of one accord."   The birds singing their matins around the poet, and the sun shining brightly through his windows stained with many a figure of poetic legend, and upon the walls painted in fine colours

" both text and gloss, and all the Rómaunt of the Rose "—
is not this a picture of Chaucer by his own hand, on which
one may love to dwell ?   And just as the poem has begun
with a touch of nature, and at the beginning of its main
action has returned to nature, so through the whole of its
course it maintains the same tone.   The sleeper awakened
—still of course in his dream—hears the sound of the
horn, and the noise of huntsmen preparing for the chase.
He rises, saddles his horse, and follows to the forest, where
the Emperor Octavian (a favourite character of Carolingian
legend, and pleasantly revived under this aspect by the
modern romanticist, Ludwig Tieck—in Chaucer's poem
probably a flattering allegory for the King) is holding his
hunt.   The deer having been started, the poet is watching
the course of the hunt, when he is approached by a dog,
which leads him to a solitary spot in a thicket among
mighty trees ; and here of a sudden he comes upon a man
in black, sitting silently by the side of a huge oak.   How
simple and how charming is the device of the faithful dog
acting as a guide into the mournful solitude of the faithful
man !   For the knight whom the poet finds thus silent and
alone, is rehearsing to himself a lay, " a manner song,"
in these words :—

> I have of sorrow so great wone,
> That joyë get I never none,
> Now that I see my lady bright,
> Which I have loved with all my might,
> Is from me dead, and is agone.
> Alas ! Death, what aileth thee
> That thou should'st not have taken me,
> When that thou took'st my lady sweet ?
> That was so fair, so fresh, so free,
> So goodë, that men may well see
> Of all goodnéss she had no meet.

Seeing the knight overcome by his grief, and on the point
of fainting, the poet accosts him, and courteously demands
his pardon for the intrusion.   Thereupon the disconsolate
mourner, touched by this token of sympathy, breaks out
into the tale of his sorrow which forms the real subject
of the poem.   It is a lament for the loss of a wife who
was hard to gain (the historical basis of this is unknown,
but great heiresses are usually hard to gain for cadets even
of royal houses), and whom, alas ! her husband was to
lose so soon after he had gained her.   Nothing could be
simpler, and nothing could be more delightful than the
Black Knight's description of his lost lady as she was at
the time when he wooed and almost despaired of winning
her.   Many of the touches in this description—and among
them some of the very happiest—are, it is true, borrowed
from the courtly Machault ; but nowhere has Chaucer
been happier, both in his appropriations and in the way
in which he has really converted them into beauties of his
own, than in this, perhaps the most lifelike picture of
maidenhood in the whole range of our literature.   Or is
not the following the portrait of an English girl, all life and
all innocence—a type not belonging, like its opposite, to
any "period" in particular—?

> I saw her dance so comelily,
> Carol and sing so sweetëly,
> And laugh, and play so womanly,
> And lookë so debónairly,
> So goodly speak and so friendlý,
> That, certes, I trow that nevermore
> Was seen so blissful a treasúre.
> For every hair upon her head,
> Sooth to say, it was not red,
> Nor yellow neither, nor brown it was,
> Methought most likë gold it was.

> And ah! what eyes my lady had,
> Debónair, goodë, glad and sad,
> Simple, of good size, not too wide.
> Thereto her look was not aside,
> Nor overthwart;

but so well set that, whoever beheld her was drawn and taken up by it, every part of him. Her eyes seemed every now and then as if she were inclined to be merciful, such was the delusion of fools : a delusion in very truth, for

> It was no counterfeited thing;
> It was her ownë pure looking;
> So the goddess, dame Natúre,
> Had made them open by measúre
> And close; for were she never so glad,
> Not foolishly her looks were spread,
> Nor wildëly, though that she play'd;
> But ever, methought, her eyen said :
> "By God, my wrath is all forgiven."

And at the same time she liked to live so happily that dulness was afraid of her; she was neither too " sober" nor too glad ; in short, no creature had ever more measure in all things.   Such was the lady whom the knight had won for himself, and whose virtues he cannot weary of rehearsing to himself or to a sympathising auditor.

> " Sir! " quoth I, " where is she now ?"
> " Now ? " quoth he, and stopped anon;
> Therewith he waxed as dead as stone,
> And said: " Alas that I was bore!
> That was the loss! and heretofore
> I told to thee what I had lost.
> Bethink thee what I said.   Thou know'st
> In sooth full little what thou meanest :
> I have lost morë than thou weenest.
> God wot, alas! right that was she."
> " Alas, sir, how ?   what may that be ? "
> " She is dead."   " Nay ? "   " Yes, by my truth ! "
> " Is that your loss ?   by God, it is ruth."

And with that word, the hunt breaking up, the knight and the poet depart to a " long castle with white walls on a rich hill" (Richmond ?), where a bell tolls and awakens the poet from his slumbers, to let him find himself lying in his bed, and the book with its legend of love and sleep resting in his hand.   One hardly knows at whom more to wonder—whether at the distinguished French scholar who sees so many trees that he cannot see a forest, and who, not content with declaring the *Book of the Duchess*, as a whole as well as in its details, a servile imitation of Machault, pronounces it at the same time one of Chaucer's feeblest productions ; or at the equally eminent English scholar who, with a flippancy which for once ceases to be amusing, opines that Chaucer ought to " have felt ashamed of himself for this most lame and impotent conclusion" of a poem " full of beauties," and ought to have been " caned for it !"   Not only was this " lame and impotent conclusion" imitated by Spenser in his lovely elegy, *Daphnaïda ;*[1] but it is the first passage in Chaucer's writings revealing, one would have thought unmistakeably, the dramatic power which was among his most characteristic gifts. The charm of this poem, notwithstanding all the artificialities with which it is overlaid, lies in its simplicity and truth to nature. A real human being is here brought before us instead of a vague abstraction ; and the glow of life is on the page, though it has to tell of death and mourning.

[1] I have been anticipated in pointing out this fact by the author of the biographical essay on *Spenser* in this series—an essay to which I cannot help taking this opportunity of offering a tribute of sincere admiration. It may not be an undesigned coincidence that the inconsolable widower of the *Daphnaïda* is named Alcýon, while Chaucer's poem begins with a reference to the myth of Ceyx and Alcyone. Sir Arthur Gorges re-appears as Alcyon in *Colin Clout's come home again.*

Chaucer is finding his strength by dipping into the true
spring of poetic inspiration; and in his dreams he is
awaking to the real capabilities of his genius. Though
he is still uncertain of himself and dependent on
others, it seems not too much to say that already in
this *Book of the Duchess* he is in some measure an original
poet.

How unconscious, at the same time, this waking must
have been is manifest from what little is known concerning the course of both his personal and his literary life
during the next few years. But there is a tide in the lives
of poets, as in those of other men, on the use or neglect of
which their future seems largely to depend. For more
reasons than one Chaucer may have been rejoiced to be
employed on the two missions abroad, which apparently
formed his chief occupation during the years 1370-1373.
In the first place, the love of books, which he so frequently
confesses, must in him have been united to a love of seeing men and cities; few are observers of character without taking pleasure in observing it. Of his literary labours
he probably took little thought during these years;
although the visit which in the course of them he paid to
Italy may be truly said to have constituted the turning-
point in his literary life. No work of his can be ascribed
to this period with certainty; none of importance has
ever been ascribed to it.

On the latter of these missions Chaucer, who left England
in the winter of 1372, visited Genoa and Florence. His
object at the former city was to negotiate concerning the settlement of a Genoese mercantile factory in one of our ports,
for in this century there already existed between Genoa
and England a commercial intercourse, which is illustrated
by the obvious etymology of the popular term *jane* occur-

ring in Chaucer in the sense of any small coin.[2] It has
been supposed that on this journey he met at Padua Petrarch, whose residence was near by at Arqua. The statement of the *Clerk* in the *Canterbury Tales* that he learnt
the story of patient Griseldis " at Padua of a worthy clerk
. . . . now dead," who was called " Francis Petrarch, the
laureate poet," may of course merely imply that Chaucer
borrowed the *Clerk's Tale* from Petrarch's Latin version
of the original by Boccaccio. But the meeting which the
expression suggests may have actually taken place, and may
have been accompanied by the most suitable conversation
which the imagination can supply ; while, on the other
hand, it is a conjecture unsupported by any evidence whatever, that a previous meeting between the pair had occurred
at Milan in 1368, when Lionel Duke of Clarence was married to his second wife with great pomp in the presence
of Petrarch and of Froissart. The really noteworthy point
is this : that while neither (as a matter of course) the
translated *Romaunt of the Rose*, nor the *Book of the
Duchess* exhibits any traces of Italian influence,. the same
assertion cannot safely be made with regard to any important poem produced by Chaucer after the date of this
Italian journey. The literature of Italy which was—and in
the first instance through Chaucer himself—to exercise
so powerful an influence upon the progress of our own,
was at last opened to him, though in what measure, and
by what gradations, must remain undecided. Before him
lay both the tragedies and the comedies, as he would have
called them, of the learned and brilliant Boccaccio—
both his epic poems and that inexhaustible treasure-house
of stories which Petrarch praised for its pious and grave

[2] " A jane" is in the *Clerk's Tale* said to be a sufficient value at
which to estimate the " stormy people."

contents, albeit they were mingled with others of undeniable jocoseness—the immortal *Decamerone*. He could
examine the refined gold of Petrarch's own verse with its
exquisite variations of its favourite pure theme and its adequate treatment of other elevated subjects ; and he might
gaze down the long vista of pictured reminiscences, grand
and sombre, called up by the mightiest Muse of the Middle
Ages, the Muse of Dante. Chaucer's genius, it may be
said at once, was not *transformed* by its contact with Italian
literature ; for a conscious desire as well as a conscientious
effort is needed for bringing about such a transformation ;
and to compare the results of his first Italian journey with
those of Goethe's pilgrimage across the Alps, for instance,
would be palpably absurd. It might even be doubted
whether for the themes which he was afterwards likely to
choose, and actually did choose, for poetic treatment the
materials at his command in French (and English) poetry
and prose would not have sufficed him. As it was, it seems
probable that he took many things from Italian literature ;
it is certain that he learnt much from it. There seems
every reason to conclude that the influence of Italian study
upon Chaucer made him more assiduous as well as more
careful in the employment of his poetic powers—more
hopeful at once, if one may so say, and more assured of
himself.

Meanwhile, soon after his return from his second foreign
mission, he was enabled to begin a more settled life at
home. He had acquitted himself to the satisfaction of
the Crown, as is shown by the grant for life of a daily
pitcher of wine, made to him on April 23rd, 1374, the
merry day of the Feast of St. George. It would of course
be a mistake to conclude, from any seeming analogies of
later times, that this grant, which was received by Chaucer

in money-value, and which seems finally to have been com-
muted for an annual payment of twenty marks, betokened
on the part of the King a spirit of patronage appropriate to
the claims of literary leisure.   How remote such a notion
was from the minds of Chaucer's employers is proved by
the terms of the patent by which, in the month of June
following, he was appointed Comptroller of the Customs
and Subsidy of wools, skins, and tanned hides in the port
of London.   This patent (doubtless according to the usual
official form) required him to write the rolls of his office
with his own hand, to be continually present there, and
to perform his duties in person and not by deputy.   By a
warrant of the same month Chaucer was granted the pension
of 10*l.* for life already mentioned, for services rendered by
him and his wife to the Duke and Duchess of Lancaster
and to the Queen ; by two successive grants of the year
1375 he received further pecuniary gratifications of a more
or less temporary nature ; and he continued to receive his
pension and allowance for robes as one of the royal esquires.
We may therefore conceive of him as now established in a
comfortable as well as seemingly secure position.   His
regular work as comptroller (of which a few scattered
documentary vestiges are preserved) scarcely offers more
points for the imagination to exercise itself upon than
Burns's excisemanship or Wordsworth's collectorship of
stamps,[3] though doubtless it must have brought him into
constant contact with merchants and with shipmen, and
may have suggested to him many a broad descriptive touch.
On the other hand, it is not necessary to be a poet to feel
something of that ineffable *ennui* of official life, which even

---

[3] It is a curious circumstance that Dryden should have received
as a reward for his political services as a satirist, an office almost
identical with Chaucer's.   But he held it for little more than a year.

the self-compensatory practice of arriving late at one's desk,
but departing from it early, can only abate, but not take
away. The passage has been often quoted in which Chaucer
half implies a feeling of the kind, and tells how he sought
recreation from what Charles Lamb would have called his
" works " at the Custom House in the reading, as we know
he did in the writing, of other books :—

> —— when thy labour done all is,
> And hast y-madë reckonings,
> Instead of rest and newë things
> Thou go'st home to thine house anon,
> And there as dumb as any stone
> Thou sittest at another book.

The house at home was doubtless that in Aldgate, of which
the lease to Chaucer, bearing date May, 1374, has been
discovered ; and to this we may fancy Chaucer walking
morning and evening from the riverside, past the Postern
Gate by the Tower.   Already, however, in 1376, the
routine of his occupations appears to have been interrupted
by his engagement on some secret service under Sir
John Burley ; and in the following year, and in 1378, he
was repeatedly abroad in the service of the Crown.   On
one of his journeys in the last-named year he was attached
in a subordinate capacity to the embassy sent to negotiate
for the marriage with the French King Charles V.'s
daughter Mary to the young King Richard II., who
had succeeded to his grandfather in 1377,—one of
those matrimonial missions which, in the days of both
Plantagenets and Tudors, formed so large a part of the
functions of European diplomacy, and which not unfrequently, as in this case at least ultimately, came to nothing.
A later journey in May of the same year took Chaucer
once more to Italy, whither he had been sent with Sir

Edward Berkeley to treat with Bernardo Visconti, joint
lord of Milan, and " scourge of Lombardy," and Sir John
Hawkwood—the former of whom finds a place in that
brief mirror of magistrates, the *Monk's Tale.* It was on
this occasion that of the two persons whom, according to
custom, Chaucer appointed to appear for him in the Courts
during his absence, one was John Gower, whose name as
that of the second poet of his age is indissolubly linked
with Chaucer's own.

So far, the new reign, which had opened amidst doubts
and difficulties for the country, had to the faithful servant
of the dynasty brought an increase of royal goodwill. In
1381—after the suppression of the great rebellion of the
villeins—King Richard II. had married the princess whose
name for a season linked together the history of two
countries the destinies of which had before that age, as
they have since, lain far asunder. Yet both Bohemia
and England, besides the nations which received from
the former the impulses communicated to it by the latter,
have reason to remember Queen Anne the learned and
the good ; since to her was probably due in the first
instance the intellectual intercourse between her native
and her adopted country. There seems every reason to
believe that it was the approach of this marriage which
Chaucer celebrated in one of the brightest and most
jocund marriage-poems ever composed by a laureate's
hand ; and if this was so, he cannot but have augmented
the favour with which he was regarded at Court. When,
therefore, by May, 1382, his foreign journeys had come
to an end, we do not wonder to find that, without being
called upon to relinquish his former office, he was appointed
in addition to the Comptrollership of the Petty Customs
in the Port of London, of which post he was allowed to

execute the duties by deputy.   In November, 1384, he
received permission to absent himself from his old comptrollership for a month, and in February, 1385, was allowed
to appoint a (permanent) deputy for this office also.
During the month of October, 1386, he sat in Parliament
at Westminster as one of the Knights of the Shire for
Kent, where we may consequently assume him to have possessed landed property.   His fortunes, therefore, at this
period had clearly risen to their height; and naturally
enough his commentators are anxious to assign to these
years the sunniest, as well as some of the most elaborate,
of his literary productions.   It is altogether probable that
the amount of leisure now at Chaucer's command enabled
him to carry into execution some of the works for which
he had gathered materials abroad and at home, and to
prepare others.   Inasmuch as it contains the passage cited
above, referring to Chaucer's official employment, his poem
called the *House of Fame* must have been written between
1374 and 1386 (when Chaucer quitted office), and probably is to be dated near the latter year.   Inasmuch as
both this poem and *Troilus and Cressid* are mentioned
in the Prologue to the *Legend of Good Women*, they must
have been written earlier than it; and the dedication of
Troilus to Gower and Strode very well agrees with the
relations known to have existed about this time between
Chaucer and his brother-poet.   Very probably all these
three works may have been put forth, in more or less rapid
succession, during this fortunate season of Chaucer's life.

A fortunate season—for in it the prince who, from
whatever cause, was indisputably the patron of Chaucer
and his wife, had, notwithstanding his unpopularity among
the lower orders, and the deep suspicion fostered by hostile
whisperings against him in his royal nephew's breast,

still contrived to hold the first place by the throne.
Though serious danger had already existed of a conflict
between the King and his uncle, yet John of Gaunt and
his Duchess Constance had been graciously dismissed
with a royal gift of golden crowns, when in July, 1386,
he took his departure for the continent, to busy himself
till his return home in November, 1389, with the affairs
of Castile, and with claims arising out of his disbursements
there.   The reasons for Chaucer's attachment to this particular patron are probably not far to seek ; on the precise
nature of the relation between them it is useless to specu-
late.   Before Wyclif's death in 1384, John of Gaunt had
openly dissociated himself from the reformer ; and whatever may have been the case in his later years, it was
certainly not as a follower of his old patron that at this
date Chaucer could have been considered a Wycliffite.

Again, this period of Chaucer's life may be called fortunate, because during it he seems to have enjoyed the only
congenial friendships of which any notice remains to us
The poem of *Troilus and Cressid* is, as was just noted,
dedicated to "the moral Gower and the philosophical
Strode."   Ralph Strode was a Dominican of Jedburgh
Abbey, a travelled scholar, whose journeys had carried
him as far as the Holy Land, and who was celebrated as a
poet in both the Latin and the English tongue, and as
a theologian and philosopher.   In connexion with speculations concerning Chaucer's relations to Wycliffism it is
worth noting that Strode, who after his return to England
was appointed to superintend several new monasteries,
was the author of a series of controversial arguments
against Wyclif.   The tradition, according to which he
taught one of Chaucer's sons, is untrustworthy.   Of John
Gower's life little more is known than of Chaucer's ; he

appears to have been a Suffolk man, holding manors in
that county as well as in Essex, but occasionally to have
resided in Kent. At the period of which we are speaking,
he may be supposed, besides his French productions,
to have already published his Latin *Vox Clamantis*—a
poem which, beginning with an allegorical narrative of
Wat Tyler's rebellion, passes on to a series of reflexions
on the causes of the movement, conceived in a spirit of
indignation against the corruptions of the Church, but
not of sympathy with Wycliffism. This is no doubt the
poem which obtained for Gower the epithet "moral"
(i. e. sententious) applied to him by Chaucer, and afterwards by Dunbar, Hawes, and Shakspere. Gower's *Vox
Clamantis* and other Latin poems (including one "against
the astuteness of the Evil One in the matter of Lollardry")
are forgotten; but his English *Confessio Amantis* has
retained its right to a place of honour in the history of
our literature. The most interesting part of this poem,
its *Prologue*, has already been cited as of value for our
knowledge of the political and social condition of its times.
It gives expression to a conservative tone and temper
of mind ; and like many conservative minds, Gower's
had adopted, or affected to adopt, the conviction that
the world was coming to an end. The cause of the
anticipated catastrophe he found in the division, or
absence of concord and love, manifest in the condition
of things around. The intensity of strife visible among
the conflicting elements of which the world, like the individual human being, is composed, too clearly announced
the imminent end of all things. Would that a new
Arion might arise to make peace where now is hate ;
but, alas! the prevailing confusion is such that God
alone may set it right. But the poem which follows

cannot be said to sustain the interest excited by this introduction. Its machinery was obviously suggested by that of the *Roman de la Rose*, though, as Warton has happily phrased it, Gower, after a fashion of his own, blends Ovid's *Art of Love* with the Breviary. The poet, wandering about in a forest, while suffering under the smart of Cupid's dart, meets Venus, the Goddess of Love, who urges him, as one upon the point of death, to make his full confession to her clerk or priest, the holy father Genius. This confession hereupon takes place by means of question and answer; both penitent and confessor entering at great length into an examination of the various sins and weaknesses of human nature, and of their remedies, and illustrating their observations by narratives, brief or elaborate, from Holy Writ, sacred legend, ancient history, and romantic story. Thus Gower's book, as he says at its close, stands " between earnest and game," and might be fairly described as a *Romaunt of the Rose*, without either the descriptive grace of Guillaume de Lorris, or the wicked wit of Jean de Meung, but full of learning and matter, and written by an author certainly not devoid of the art of telling stories. The mind of this author was thoroughly didactic in its bent; for the beauty of nature he has no real feeling, and though his poem, like so many of Chaucer's, begins in the month of May, he is (unnecessarily) careful to tell us that his object in going forth was not to "sing with the birds." He could not, like Chaucer, transfuse old things into new, but there is enough in his character as a poet to explain the friendship between the pair, of which we hear at the very time when Gower was probably preparing his *Confessio Amantis* for publication.

They are said afterwards to have become enemies; but

in the absence of any real evidence to that effect we
cannot believe Chaucer to have been likely to quarrel with
one whom he had certainly both trusted and admired.
Nor had literary life in England already advanced to a
stage of development of which, as in the Elizabethan and
Augustan ages, literary jealousy was an indispensable
accompaniment. Chaucer is supposed to have attacked
Gower in a passage of the *Canterbury Tales*, where he
incidentally declares his dislike (in itself extremely com-
mendable) of a particular kind of sensational stories, in-
stancing the subject of one of the numerous tales in the
Confessio Amantis. There is, however, no reason whatever for supposing Chaucer to have here intended a
reflection on his brother poet, more especially as the *Man
of Law*, after uttering the censure, relates, though probably not from Gower, a story on a subject of a different
kind likewise treated by him. It is scarcely more sus-
picious that when Gower, in a second edition of his chief
work, dedicated in 1393 to Henry, Earl of Derby.
(afterwards Henry IV.), judiciously omitted the exordium
and altered the close of the first edition, both of which were
complimentary to Richard II., he left out, together with
its surrounding context, a passage conveying a friendly
challenge to Chaucer as a " disciple and poet of the God
of Love."

In any case there could have been no political difference
between them, for Chaucer was at all times in favour with
the House of Lancaster, towards whose future head Gower
so early contrived to assume a correct attitude. To him
—a man of substance, with landed property in three
counties—the rays of immediate court-favour were probably of less importance than to Chaucer; but it is not
necessity only which makes courtiers of so many of us:

some are born to the vocation, and Gower strikes one as naturally more prudent and cautious—in short, more of a politic personage—than Chaucer. He survived him eight years—a blind invalid, in whose mind at least we may hope nothing dimmed or blurred the recollection of a friend to whom he owes much of his fame.

In a still nearer relationship,—on which the works of Chaucer that may certainly or probably be assigned to this period throw some light,—it seems impossible to describe him as having been fortunate. Whatever may have been the date and circumstances of his marriage, it seems, at all events in its later years, not to have been a happy one. The allusions to Chaucer's personal experience of married life in both *Troilus and Cressid* and the *House of Fame* are not of a kind to be entirely explicable by that tendency to make a mock of women and of marriage, which has frequently been characteristic of satirists, and which was specially popular in an age cherishing the wit of Jean de Meung, and complacently corroborating its theories from naughty Latin fables, French *fabliaux*, and Italian *novelle*. Both in *Troilus and Cressid* and in the *House of Fame* the poet's tone, when he refers to himself, is generally dolorous; but while both poems contain unmistakeable references to the joylessness of his own married life, in the latter he speaks of himself as " suffering debonairly," —or, as we should say, putting a good face upon—a state " desperate of all bliss." And it is a melancholy though half sarcastic glimpse into his domestic privacy which he incidentally, and it must be allowed rather unnecessarily, gives in the following passage of the same poem :—

> " Awake !" to me he said,
> In voice and tone the very same
> *That useth one whom I could name;*

> And with that voice, sooth to say (n)
> My mind returned to me again;
> For it was goodly said to me;
> So was it never wont to be.

In other words, the kindness of the voice reassured him
that it was *not* the same as that which he was wont to hear
close to his pillow ! Again, the entire tone of the Prologue
to the *Legend of Good Women* is not that of a happy lover ;
although it would be pleasant enough, considering that
the lady who imposes on the poet the penalty of celebrat-
ing *good* women is Alcestis, the type of faithful wifehood,
to interpret the poem as not only an *amende honorable* to
the female sex in general, but a token of reconciliation to
the poet's wife in particular. Even in the joyous *Assembly
of Fowls*, a marriage-poem, the same discord already makes
itself heard ; for it cannot be without meaning that in his
dream the poet is told by "African,"—

> —— thou of love hast lost thy taste, I guess,
> As sick men have of sweet and bitterness;

and that he confesses for himself that, though he has read
much of love, he knows not of it by experience. While,
however, we reluctantly accept the conclusion that Chaucer
was unhappy as a husband, we must at the same time decline, because the husband was a poet, and one of the most
genial of poets, to cast all the blame upon the wife, and to
write her down a shrew. It is unfortunate, no doubt, but
it is likewise inevitable, that at so great a distance of time
the rights and wrongs of a conjugal disagreement or
estrangement cannot with safety be adjusted. Yet again,
because we refuse to blame Philippa, we are not obliged
to blame Chaucer. At the same time it must not be con-
cealed, that his name occurs in the year 1380 in connexion
with a legal process of which the most obvious, though

not the only possible, explanation is that he had been
guilty of a grave infidelity towards his wife. Such dis-
coveries as this last we might be excused for wishing
unmade.

Considerable uncertainty remains with regard to the
dates of the poems belonging to this seemingly, in all
respects but one, fortunate period of Chaucer's life. Of
one of these works, however, which has had the curious fate
to be dated and re-dated by a succession of happy conjectures, the last and happiest of all may be held to have
definitively fixed the occasion. This is the charming poem
called the *Assembly of Fowls*, or *Parliament of Birds*—a
production which seems so English, so fresh from nature's
own inspiration, so instinct with the gaiety of Chaucer's
own heart, that one is apt to overlook in it the undeniable
vestiges of foreign influences, both French and Italian.
At its close the poet confesses that he is always reading,
and therefore hopes that he may at last read something
"so to fare the better." But with all this evidence of
study the *Assembly of Fowls* is chiefly interesting as showing how Chaucer had now begun to select as well as to
assimilate his loans; how, while he was still moving along
well-known tracks, his eyes were joyously glancing to the
right and the left; and how the source of most of his
imagery at all events he already found in the merry
England around him, even as he had chosen for his subject
one of real national interest.

Anne of Bohemia, daughter of the great Emperor
Charles IV., and sister of King Wenceslas, had been successively betrothed to a Bavarian prince and to a Margrave
of Meissen, before—after negotiations which, according
to Froissart, lasted a year—her hand was given to the
young King Richard II. of England. This sufficiently

explains the general scope of the *Assembly of Fowls*, an
allegorical poem written on or about St. Valentine's Day,
1381—eleven months or nearly a year after which date
the marriage took place.   On the morning sacred to lovers
the poet (in a dream, of course, and this time conducted
by the arch-dreamer Scipio in person) enters a garden containing in it the temple of the god of Love, and filled with
inhabitants mythological and allegorical.   Here he sees
the noble goddess Nature, seated upon a hill of flowers, and
around her " all the fowls that be," assembled as by time-
honoured custom on St. Valentine's Day, " when every
fowl comes there to choose her mate."   Their huge noise
and hubbub is reduced to order by Nature, who assigns
to each fowl its proper place—the birds of prey highest;
then those that eat according to natural inclination—

> —worm or thing of which I tell no tale;

then those that live by seed ; and the various members of
the several classes are indicated with amusing vivacity and
point, from the royal eagle " that with his sharp look
pierceth the sun," and "other eagles of a lower kind"
downwards.   We can only find room for a portion of the
company :—

> The sparrow, Venus' son; the nightingale
> That clepeth forth the freshë leavës new ;
> The swallow, murd'rer of the beës small,
> That honey make of flowers fresh of hue ;
> The wedded turtle, with his heartë true ;
> The peacock, with his angels' feathers bright,
> The pheasant, scorner of the cock by night.
>
> The waker goose, the cuckoo, ever unkind ;
> The popinjay, full of delícacy ;
> The drake, destrôyer of his ownë kind ;
> The stork, avenger of adultery ;
> The cormorant, hot and full of gluttony ;

> The crows and ravens with their voice of care;
> And the throstle old, and the frostý fieldfáre.

Naturalists must be left to explain some of these epithets
and designations, not all of which rest on allusions as
easily understood as that recalling the goose's exploit
on the Capitol; but the vivacity of the whole description
speaks for itself. One is reminded of Aristophanes'
feathered chorus; but birds are naturally the delight of
poets, and were befriended by Dante himself.

Hereupon the action of the poem opens. A female
eagle is wooed by three suitors—all eagles; but among
them the first, or royal eagle, discourses in the manner
most likely to conciliate favour. Before the answer is
given, a pause furnishes an opportunity to the other
fowls for delighting in the sound of their own voices,
Dame Nature proposing that each class of birds shall,
through the beak of its representative "agitator," express its opinion on the problem before the assembly.
There is much humour in the readiness of the goose to
rush in with a ready-made resolution, and in the smart
reproof administered by the sparrow-hawk amidst the up-
roar of " the gentle fowls all." At last Nature silences
the tumult, and the lady-eagle delivers her answer, to the
effect that she cannot make up her mind for a year to
come; but inasmuch as Nature has advised her to choose
the royal eagle, his is clearly the most favourable prospect.
Whereupon, after certain fowls had sung a roundel, "as
was always the usance," the assembly, like some human
Parliaments, breaks up with shouting; [4] and the dreamer
awakes to resume his reading.

> [4] Than all the birdis song with sic a schout
> That I annone awoik quhair that I lay.
>   DUNBAR, *The Thrissill and the Rois.*

Very possibly the *Assembly of Fowls* was at no great interval of time either followed or preceded by two poems of far inferior interest—the *Complaint of Mars* (apparently afterwards amalgamated with that of *Venus*), which is supposed to be sung by a bird on St. Valentine's morning, and the fragment *Of Queen Anelida and false Arcite*. There are, however, reasons which make a less early date probable in the case of the latter production, the history of the origin and purpose of which can hardly be said as yet to be removed out of the region of mere speculation.   In any case, neither of these poems can be looked upon as preparations, on Chaucer's part, for the longer work on which he was to expend so much labour ; but in a sense this description would apply to the translation which, probably before he wrote *Troilus and Cressid*, certainly before he wrote the Prologue to the *Legend of Good Women*, he made of the famous Latin work of Boëthius, "the just man in prison," on the *Consolation of Philosophy*.   This book was, and very justly so, one of the favourite manuals of the Middle Ages, and a treasure-house of religious wisdom to centuries of English writers. "Boice of Consolacioun" is cited in the *Romaunt of the Rose ;* and the list of passages imitated by Chaucer from the martyr of Catholic orthodoxy and Roman freedom of speech is exceedingly long.   Among them are the ever-recurring diatribe against the fickleness of fortune, and (through the medium of Dante) the reflection on the distinction between gentle birth and a gentle life.   Chaucer's translation was not made at second-hand ; if not always easy it is conscientious, and interpolated with numerous glosses and explanations thought necessary by the translator.   The metre of *The Former Life* he at one time or another turned into verse of his own.

Perhaps the most interesting of the quotations made in Chaucer's poems from Boëthius occurs in his *Troilus and Cressid,* one of the many mediæval versions of an episode engrafted by the lively fancy of an Anglo-Norman *trouvère* upon the deathless, and in its literary variations incomparably luxuriant, growth of the story of Troy. On Benoît de Sainte-Maure's poem Guido de Colonna founded his Latin-prose romance; and this again, after being reproduced in languages and by writers almost innumerable, served Boccaccio as the foundation of his poem *Filostrato* —i. e. the victim of love. All these works, together with Chaucer's *Troilus and Cressid,* with Lydgate's *Troy-Book,* with Henryson's *Testament of Cressid* (and in a sense even with Shakspere's drama on the theme of Chaucer's poem), may be said to belong to the second cycle of modern versions of the tale of Troy divine. Already their earlier predecessors had gone far astray from Homer, of whom they only knew by hearsay, relying for their facts on late Latin epitomes, which freely mutilated and perverted the Homeric narrative in favour of the Trojans—the supposed ancestors of half the nations of Europe. Accordingly, Chaucer, in a well-known passage in his *House of Fame,* regrets, with sublime coolness, how " one said that Homer " wrote " lies,"

> Feigning in his poetries
> And was to Greekës favouráble.
> Therefore held he it but fable.

But the courtly poets of the romantic age of literature went a step further, and added a mediæval colouring all their own. One converts the Sibyl into a nun, and makes her admonish Æneas to tell his beads. Another—it is Chaucer's successor Lydgate—introduces Priam's sons exercising

their bodies in tournaments and their minds in the glorious
play of chess, and causes the memory of Hector to be consecrated by the foundation of a chantry of priests who are
to pray for the repose of his soul. A third finally con-
demns the erring Cressid to be stricken with leprosy, and
to wander about with cup and clapper, like the unhappy
lepers in the great cities of the Middle Ages. Everything,
in short, is transfused by the spirit of the adapters' own
times; and so far are these writers from any weakly sense
of anachronism in describing Troy as if it were a moated
and turreted city of the later Middle Ages, that they are
only careful now and then to protest their own truthfulness when anything in their narrative seems *unlike* the
days in which they write.

But Chaucer, though his poem is, to start with, only an
English reproduction of an Italian version of a Latin
translation of a French poem, and though in most respects
it shares the characteristic features of the body of poetic
fiction to which it belongs, is far from being a mere
translator.   Apart from several remarkable reminiscences
introduced by Chaucer from Dante, as well as from the
irrepressible *Romaunt of the Rose*, he has changed his
original in points which are not mere matters of detail or
questions of convenience.   In accordance with the essentially dramatic bent of his own genius, some of these
changes have reference to the aspect of the characters and
the conduct of the plot, as well as to the whole spirit of the
conception of the poem.   Cressid (who, by the way, is a
widow at the outset—whether she had children or not,
Chaucer nowhere found stated, and therefore leaves undecided) may at first sight strike the reader as a less consistent character in Chaucer than in Boccaccio.   But there
is true art in the way in which, in the English poem, our

sympathy is first aroused for the heroine, whom, in the
end, we cannot but condemn.   In Boccaccio, Cressid is
fair and false—one of those fickle creatures with whom
Italian literature, and Boccaccio in particular, so largely
deal, and whose presentment merely repeats to us the old
cynical half-truth as to woman's weakness.   The English
poet, though he does not pretend that his heroine was
"religious" (i.e. a nun to whom earthly love is a sin),
endears her to us from the first; so much that " O the
pity of it" seems the hardest verdict we can ultimately
pass upon her conduct.   How, then, is the catastrophe of
the action, the falling away of Cressid from her truth to
Troilus, poetically explained ? By an appeal—pedantically
put, perhaps, and as it were dragged in violently by means
of a truncated quotation from Boëthius—to the fundamental difficulty concerning the relations between poor
human life and the government of the world.   This, it
must be conceded, is a considerably deeper problem than
the nature of woman.   Troilus and Cressid, the hero sinned
against and the sinning heroine, are the *victims of Fate*.
Who shall cast a stone against those who are, but like the
rest of us, predestined to their deeds and to their doom ;
since the co-existence of free-will with predestination does
not admit of proof?   This solution of the conflict may be
morally as well as theologically unsound ; it certainly is
æsthetically faulty; but it is the reverse of frivolous or
commonplace.

   Or let us turn from Cressid, "matchless in beauty,"
and warm with sweet life, but not ignoble even in the
season of her weakness, to another personage of the poem.
In itself the character of Pandarus is one of the most
revolting which imagination can devise ; so much so that
the name has become proverbial for the most despicable

of human types. With Boccaccio Pandarus is Cressid's
cousin and Troilus' youthful friend, and there is no intention of making him more offensive than are half the con-
fidants of amorous heroes. But Chaucer sees his dramatic
opportunity; and without painting black in black and
creating a monster of vice, he invents a good-natured and
loquacious, elderly go-between, full of proverbial philosophy and invaluable experience—a genuine light comedy
character for all times. How admirably this Pandarus
practises as well as preaches his art; using the hospitable
Deiphobus and the queenly Helen as unconscious instru-
ments in his intrigue for bringing the lovers together:—

> She came to dinner in her plain intent;
> But God and Pandar wist what all this meant.

Lastly, considering the extreme length of Chaucer's
poem, and the very simple plot of the story which it tells,
one cannot fail to admire the skill with which the conduct
of its action is managed. In Boccaccio the earlier part of
the story is treated with brevity, while the conclusion, after
the catastrophe has occurred and the main interest has
passed, is long drawn out. Chaucer dwells at great length
upon the earlier and pleasing portion of the tale, more
especially on the falling in love of Cressid, which is worked
out with admirable naturalness. But he comparatively
hastens over its pitiable end—the fifth and last book of his
poem corresponding to not less than four cantos of the
Filostrato. In Chaucer's hands, therefore, the story is a
real love-story, and the more that we are led to rejoice
with the lovers in their bliss, the more our compassion is
excited by the lamentable end of so much happiness; and
we feel at one with the poet, who, after lingering over the
happiness of which he has in the end to narrate the fall, as

it were unwillingly proceeds to accomplish his task, and
bids his readers be wroth with the destiny of his heroine
rather than with himself. His own heart, he says, bleeds
and his pen quakes to write what must be written of the
falsehood of Cressid, which was her doom.

Chaucer's nature, however tried, was unmistakeably one
gifted with the blessed power of easy self-recovery. Though
it was in a melancholy vein that he had begun to write
Troilus and Cressid, he had found opportunities enough
in the course of the poem for giving expression to the fresh
vivacity and playful humour which are justly reckoned
among his chief characteristics. And thus, towards its
close, we are not surprised to find him apparently looking
forward to a sustained effort of a kind more congenial to
himself. He sends forth his "little book, his little
tragedy," with the prayer that, before he dies, God his
Maker may send him might to "make some comedy."
If the poem called the *House of Fame* followed upon
Troilus and Cressid (the order of succession may, however,
have been the reverse), then, although the poet's own
mood had little altered, yet he had resolved upon essay-
ing a direction which he rightly felt to be suitable to his
genius.

The *House of Fame* has not been distinctly traced to
any one foreign source; but the influence of both Petrarch
and Dante, as well as that of classical authors, are
clearly to be traced in the poem. And yet this work,
Chaucer's most ambitious attempt in poetical allegory,
may be described not only as in the main due to an original
conception, but as representing the results of the writer's
personal experience. All things considered, it is the production of a man of wonderful reading, and shows that
Chaucer's was a mind interested in the widest variety of

subjects, which drew no invidious distinctions, such as
we moderns are prone to insist upon, between Arts and
Science, but (notwithstanding an occasional deprecatory
modesty) eagerly sought to familiarise itself with the
achievements of both: In a passage concerning the men
of letters who had found a place in the *House of Fame*,
he displays not only an acquaintance with the names
of several ancient classics, but also a keen appre-
ciation, now and then perhaps due to instinct, of their
several characteristics. Elsewhere he shows his interest
in scientific inquiry by references to such matters as
the theory of sound and the Arabic system of numera-
tion ; while the Mentor of the poem, the Eagle, openly
boasts his powers of clear scientific demonstration, in
averring that he can speak "lewdly" (i. e. popularly)
"to a lewd man." The poem opens with a very fresh
and lively discussion of the question of dreams in general
—a semi-scientific subject which much occupied Chaucer,
and upon which even Pandarus and the wedded couple of
the *Nun's Priest's Tale* expend their philosophy.

Thus, besides giving evidence of considerable information and study, the *House of Fame* shows Chaucer to have
been gifted with much natural humour. Among its happy
touches are the various rewards bestowed by Fame upon
the claimants for her favour, including the ready grant of
evil fame to those who desire it (a bad name, to speak
colloquially, is to be had for the asking) ; and the wonderful paucity of those who wish their good works to
remain in obscurity and to be their own reward, but then
Chaucer was writing in the Middle Ages. And as pointing in a direction which the author of the poem was sub-
sequently to follow out, we may also specially notice the
company thronging the House of Rumour : shipmen and

pilgrims, the two most numerous kinds of travellers in
Chaucer's age, fresh from seaport and sepulchre, with scrips
brimful of unauthenticated intelligence. In short, this
poem offers in its details much that is characteristic of its
author's genius; while, as a whole, its abrupt termination
notwithstanding, it leaves the impression of completeness.
The allegory, simple and clear in construction, fulfils the
purpose for which it was devised; the conceptions upon
which it is based are neither idle, like many of those in
Chaucer's previous allegories, nor are they so artificial and
far-fetched as to fatigue instead of stimulating the mind.
Pope, who reproduced parts of the *House of Fame* in a
loose paraphrase, in attempting to improve the construction of Chaucer's work, only mutilated it. As it stands,
it is clear and digestible; and how many allegories, one
may take leave to ask, in our own allegory-loving literature or in any other, merit the same commendation? For
the rest, Pope's own immortal *Dunciad*, though doubtless
more immediately suggested by a personal satire of Dryden's, is in one sense a kind of travesty of the *House of
Fame*,—a *House of Infamy*.

In the theme of this poem there was undoubtedly something that could hardly fail to humour the half-melancholy
mood in which it was manifestly written. Are not, the
poet could not but ask himself, all things vanity; " as men
say, what may ever last ?" Yet the subject brought its
consolation likewise. Patient labour, such as this poem
attests, is the surest road to that enduring fame, which is
" conserved with the shade;" and awaking from his vision,
Chaucer takes leave of the reader with a resolution already
habitual to him—to read more and more, instead of resting
satisfied with the knowledge he has already acquired.
And in the last of the longer poems which seem assignable

to this period of his life, he proves that one Latin poet at least—Venus' clerk, whom in the *House of Fame* he beheld standing on a pillar of her own Cyprian metal—had been read as well as celebrated by him.

Of this poem, the fragmentary *Legend of Good Women*, the *Prologue* possesses a peculiar biographical as well as literary interest. In his personal feelings on the subject of love and marriage, Chaucer had, when he wrote this *Prologue*, evidently almost passed even beyond the sarcastic stage. And as a poet he was now clearly conscious of being no longer a beginner, no longer a learner only, but one whom his age knew, and in whom it took a critical interest. The list including most of his undoubted works, which he here recites, shows of itself that those already spoken of in the foregoing pages were by this time known to the world, together with two of the *Canterbury Tales*, which had either been put forth independently, or (as seems much less probable) had formed the first instalment of his great work. A further proof of the relatively late date of this *Prologue* occurs in the contingent offer which it makes of the poem to "the Queen," who can be no other than Richard II.'s young consort Anne. At the very outset we find Chaucer as it were reviewing his own literary position —and doing so in the spirit of an author who knows very well what is said against him, who knows very well what there is in what is said against him, and who yet is full of that true self-consciousness which holds to its course—not recklessly and ruthlessly, not with a contempt for the feelings and judgments of his fellow-creatures, but with a serene trust in the justification ensured to every honest endeavour. The principal theme of his poems had hitherto been the passion of love,

H

and woman who is the object of the love of man. Had
he not, the superfine critics of his day may have asked—
steeped as they were in the artificiality and florid extravagance of chivalry in the days of its decline, and
habituated to mistranslating earthly passion into the
phraseology of religious devotion—had he not debased
the passion of love, and defamed its object? Had he not
begun by translating the wicked satire of Jean de Meung,
"a heresy against the law" of Love, and had he not, by
cynically painting in his Cressid a picture of woman's
perfidy, encouraged men to be less faithful to women

> That be as true as ever was any steel?

In Chaucer's way of meeting this charge, which he
emphasises by putting it in the mouth of the God of Love
himself, it is, to be sure, difficult to recognise any very
deeply penitent spirit. He mildly wards off the reproach,
sheltering himself behind his defender, the "lady in
green," who afterwards proves to be herself that type of
womanly and wifely fidelity unto death, the true and
brave Alcestis. And even in the body of the poem one
is struck by a certain perfunctoriness, not to say flippancy,
in the way in which its moral is reproduced. The wrathful
invective against the various classical followers of Lamech,
the maker of tents,[5] wears no aspect of deep moral

---

[5] Lamech, Chaucer tells us in *Queen Annelida and the false
Arcite*, was the

> first father that began
> The love of two, and was in bigamy.

This poem seems designed to illustrate much the same moral
as that enforced by the *Legend of Good Women*—a moral which,
by-the-bye, is already foreshadowed towards the close of *Troilus
and Cressid*, where Chaucer speaks of

> women that betrayèd be
> Through falsë folk, (God give them sorrow, amen !)
>   [That

indignation; and it is not precisely the voice of a
repentant sinner which concludes the pathetic story of the
betrayal of Phillis with the adjuration to ladies in
general :—

> Beware ye women of your subtle foe,
> Since yet this day men may example see ;
> And as in love trust ye no man but me.

At the same time the poet lends an attentive ear, as
genius can always afford to do, to a criticism of his
shortcomings, and readily accepts the sentence pronounced
by Alcestis that he shall write a legend of *good* women,
both maidens and also wives, that were

> true in loving all their lives.

And thus, with the courage of a good or at all events
easy conscience, he sets about his task which unfortunately
—it is conjectured by reason of domestic calamities,
probably including the death of his wife—remained, or at
least has come down to us unfinished. We have only
nine of the nineteen stories which he appears to have
intended to present (though indeed a manuscript of
Henry IV.'s reign quotes Chaucer's book of " xxv good
women"). It is by no means necessary to suppose that all
these nine stories were written continuously ; maybe, too,
Chaucer, with all his virtuous intentions, grew tired of his
rather monotonous scheme, at a time when he was beginning to busy himself with stories meant to be fitted into the

> That with their greatë wit and subtlety
> Betray you ; and 'tis this that moveth me
> To speak; and, in effect, you all I pray :
> Beware of men, and hearken what I say.

more liberal framework of the *Canterbury Tales.* All these
illustrations of female constancy are of classical origin, as
Chaucer is glad to make known, and most of them are
taken from Ovid.   But though the thread of the English
poet's narratives is supplied by such established favourites
as the stories of Cleopatra the Martyr Queen of Egypt,
of Thisbe of Babylon the Martyr, and of Dido to whom
" Æneas was forsworn," yet he by no means slavishly
adheres to his authorities, but alters or omits in accordance
with the design of his book.   Thus, for instance, we read
of Medea's desertion by Jason, but hear nothing of her as
the murderess of her children ; while, on the other hand,
the tragedy of Dido is enhanced by pathetic additions
not to be found in Virgil.   Modern taste may dislike the
way in which this poem mixes up the terms and ideas of
Christian martyrology with classical myths, and as " the
Legend of the Saints of Cupid " assumes the character of
a kind of calendar of women canonised by reason of their
faithfulness to earthly love.   But obviously this is a
method of treatment belonging to an age, not to a single
poem or poet.   Chaucer's artistic judgment in the selection
and arrangement of his themes, the wonderful vivacity
and true pathos with which he turns upon Tarquin or
Jason as if they had personally offended him, and
his genuine flow of feeling not only *for* but *with* his
unhappy heroines, add a new charm to the old familiar
faces.   Proof is thus furnished, if any proof were needed,
that no story interesting in itself is too old to admit of
being told again by a poet; in Chaucer's version Ovid
loses something in polish, but nothing in pathos ; and the
breezy freshness of nature seems to be blowing through
tales which became the delight of a nation's, as they have
been that of many a man's, youth.

A single passage must suffice to illustrate the style of
the *Legend of Good Women;* and it shall be the lament
of Ariadne, the concluding passage of the story which
is the typical tale of desertion, though not, as it remains in Chaucer, of desertion unconsoled. It will be
seen how far the English poet's vivacity is from being
extinguished by the pathos of the situation described by
him.

> Right in the dawëning awaketh she,
> And gropeth in the bed, and found right naught.
> " Alas," quoth she, " that ever I was wrought!
> I am betrayèd!" and her hair she rent,
> And to the strandë barefoot fast she went,
> And criedë : " Theseus, mine heartë sweet !
> Where be ye, that I may not with you meet ?
> And mightë thus by beastës been y-slain !"
> The hollow rockës answered her again.
> No man she sawë ; and yet shone the moon,
> And high upon a rock she wentë soon,
> And saw his bargë sailing in the sea.
> Cold waxed her heart, and right thus saidë she :
> "Meeker than ye I find the beastës wild !"
> (Hath he not sin that he her thus beguiled ?)
> She cried, " O turn again for ruth and sin,
> Thy bargë hath not all thy meinie in."
> Her kerchief on a polë stickèd she,
> Askancë, that he should it well y-see,
> And should remember that she was behind,
> And turn again, and on the strand her find.
> But all for naught ; his way he is y-gone,
> And down she fell aswoonë on a stone ;
> And up she rose, and kissed, in all her care,
> The steppës of his feet remaining there ;
> And then unto her bed she speaketh so :
> "Thou bed," quoth she, " that hast receivèd two,
> Thou shalt answér for two, and not for one ;
> Where is the greater part away y-gone ?
> Alas, what shall I wretched wight become ?
> For though so be no help shall hither come,

> Home to my country dare I not for dread,
> I can myselfë in this case not rede."
> Why should I tell more of her cómplaining ?
> It is so long it were a heavy thing.
> In her Epistle Naso telleth all.
> But shortly to the endë tell I shall.
> The goddës have her holpen for pitý,
> And in the sign of Taurus men may see
> The stonës of her crown all shining clear.
> I will no further speak of this mattér.
> But thus these falsë lovers can beguile
> Their truë love; the devil quite him his while!

Manifestly, then, in this period of his life—if a chronology which is in a great measure conjectural may be accepted—Chaucer had been a busy worker, and his pen had covered many a page with the results of his rapid productivity.   Perhaps, his *Words unto his own Scrivener*, which we may fairly date about this time, were rather too hard on "Adam."   Authors *are* often hard on persons who have to read their handiwork professionally; but in the interest of posterity poets may be permitted an execration or two against whosoever changes their words as well as against whosoever moves their bones :—

> Adam Scrivener, if ever it thee befall
> *Boece* or *Troilus* to write anew,
> Under thy long locks may'st thou have the scall,
> If thou my writing copy not more true!
> So oft a day I must thy work renew,
> It to correct and eke to rub and scrape;
> And all is through thy negligence and rape.

How far the manuscript of the *Canterbury Tales* had already progressed is uncertain; the *Prologue* to the *Legend of Good Women* mentions the *Love of Palamon and Arcite*—an earlier version of the *Knight's Tale*, if not identical with it—and a *Life of Saint Cecilia* which is preserved, apparently without alteration, in the *Second Nun's Tale.* Possibly other stories had been already added to these, and the *Prologue* written—but this is more than can be asserted with safety. Who shall say whether, if the stream of prosperity had continued to flow, on which the bark of Chaucer's fortunes had for some years been borne along, he might not have found leisure and impulse sufficient for completing his masterpiece, or at all events for advancing it near to completion? That his powers declined with his years is a conjecture which it would be difficult to support by satisfactory evidence; though it seems natural enough to assume that he wrote the best of his *Canterbury Tales* in his best days. Troubled times we know to have been in store for him. The reverse in his fortunes may perhaps fail to call forth in us the sympathy which we feel for Milton in his old age doing battle against a Philistine reaction, or for Spenser overwhelmed with calamities at the end of a life full of bitter disappointment. But at least we may look upon it with the respectful pity which we entertain for Ben Jonson groaning in the midst of his literary honours under that *dura rerum necessitas,* which is rarely more a matter of indifference to poets than it is to other men.

In 1386, as already noted, Chaucer, while continuing to hold both his offices at the Customs, had taken his seat in Parliament as one of the knights of the shire of Kent. He had attained to this honour during the absence in Spain of his patron the Duke of Lancaster, though probably he had been elected in the interest of that prince. But John of Gaunt's influence was inevitably reduced to nothing during his absence, and no doubt King Richard now hoped to be a free agent. But he very speedily found that the hand of his younger uncle, Thomas Duke of

Gloucester, was heavier upon him than that of the elder.
The Parliament of which Chaucer was a member was the
assembly which boldly confronted the autocratical tendencies of Richard II., and after overthrowing the Chan-
cellor, Michael de la Pole, Earl of Suffolk, forced upon the
king a Council controlling the administration of affairs.
Concerning the acts of this Council, of which Gloucester
was the leading member, little or nothing is known, except
that in financial matters it attempted, after the manner
of new brooms, to sweep clean. Soon the attention of
Gloucester and his following was occupied by subjects
more absorbing than a branch of reform fated to be treated
fitfully.   In this instance the new administration had
as usual demanded its victims—and among their number
was Chaucer.   For it can hardly be a mere coincidence
that by the beginning of December in this year, 1386,
Chaucer had lost one, and by the middle of the same
month the other, of his comptrollerships. At the same
time, it would be presumptuously unfair to conclude that
misconduct of any kind on his part had been the reason
of his removal. The explanation usually given is that he
fell as an adherent of John of Gaunt; perhaps a safer
way of putting the matter would be to say that John
of Gaunt was no longer in England to protect him. Inasmuch as even reforming Governments are occasionally
as anxious about men as they are about measures, Chaucer's
posts may have been wanted for nominees of the Duke of
Gloucester and his Council—such as it is probably no
injustice to Masters Adam Yerdely and Henry Gisors
(who respectively succeeded Chaucer in his two offices) to
suppose them to have been.   Moreover, it is just possible
that Chaucer was the reverse of a *persona grata* to Gloucester's faction on account of the Comptroller's previous

official connexion with Sir Nicholas Brembre, who, besides being hated in the city, had been accused of seeking
to compass the deaths of the Duke and of some of his adherents.   In any case, it is noticeable that four months
before the return to England of the Duke of Lancaster,
i.e. in July, 1389, Chaucer was appointed Clerk of the
King's Works at Westminster, the Tower, and a large
number of other royal manors or tenements, including
(from 1390 at all events) St. George's Chapel, Windsor.
In this office he was not ill-paid, receiving two shillings a
day in money, and very possibly perquisites in addition,
besides being allowed to appoint a deputy.   Inasmuch as
in the summer of the year 1389 King Richard had assumed
the reins of government in person, while the ascendancy of
Gloucester was drawing to a close, we may conclude the
King to have been personally desirous to provide for a faithful and attached servant of his house, for whom he had
had reason to feel a personal liking.   It would be specially
pleasing, were we able to connect with Chaucer's restora-
tion to official employment the high-minded Queen Anne,
whose impending betrothal he had probably celebrated
in one poem, and whose patronage he had claimed for
another.

The Clerkship of the King's Works to which Chaucer
was appointed, seems to have been but a temporary office ;
or at all events he only held it for rather less than two
years, during part of which he performed its duties by
deputy.   Already, however, before his appointment to
this post, he had certainly become involved in difficulties.
For in May, 1388, we find his pensions, at his own request,
assigned to another person (John Scalby)—a statement implying that he had raised money on them which he could
only pay by making over the pensions themselves.   Very

possibly, too, he had, before his dismissal from his comptrollerships, been subjected to an enquiry which, if it did
not touch his honour, at all events gave rise to very natural apprehensions on the part of himself and his friends.
There is accordingly much probability in the conjecture
which ascribes to this season of peril and pressure the
composition of the following justly famous stanzas entitled
Good Counsel of Chaucer :—

> Flee from the press, and dwell with soothfastness ;
> Sufficë thee thy good, though it be small ;
> For hoard hath hate, and climbing tickleness :
> Press hath envý, and wealth is blinded all.
> Savour no more than thee behovë shall ;.
> Do well thyself that other folk canst rede ;
> And truth thee shall deliver, it is no dread.
>
> Painë thee not each crooked to redress
> In trust of her [6] that turneth as a ball.
> Greatë rest stands in little business.
> Beware also to spurn against a nail.
> Strive not as doth a pitcher with a wall.
> Deemë thyself that deemest others' deed ;
> And truth thee shall deliver, it is no dread.
>
> That thee is sent receive in buxomness ;
> The wrestling of this world asketh a fall.
> Here is no home, here is but wilderness.
> Forth, pilgrimë ! forth, beast, out of thy stall !
> Look up on high, and thankë God of all.
> Waivë thy lust, and let thy ghost thee lead,
> And truth shall thee deliver, it is no dread.

Misfortunes, it is said, never come alone ; and whatever
view may be taken as to the nature of the relations between Chaucer and his wife, her death cannot have left
him untouched. From the absence of any record as to
the payment of her pension after June, 1387, this event

[6] Fortune.

is presumed to have taken place in the latter half of that
year.   More than this cannot safely be conjectured ;
but it remains *possible* that the *Legend of Good Women*
and its *Prologue* formed a peace-offering to one whom
Chaucer may have loved again after he had lost her, though
without thinking of her as of his " late departed saint."
Philippa Chaucer had left behind her a son of the name
of Lewis ; and it is pleasing to find the widower in the
year 1391 (the year in which he lost his Clerkship of the
Works) attending to the boy's education, and supplying
him with the intellectual " bread and milk" suitable for
his tender age in the shape of a popular treatise on a
subject which has at all times excited the intelligent
curiosity of the young.   The treatise *On the Astrolabe*,
after describing the instrument itself, and showing how
to work it, proceeded, or was intended to proceed, to
fulfil the purposes of a general astronomical manual ; but,
like other and more important works of its author, it has
come down to us in an uncompleted, or at all events
incomplete, condition.   What there is of it was, as a
matter of course, not original—popular scientific books
rarely are.   The little treatise, however, possesses a double
interest for the student of Chaucer.   In the first place it
shows explicitly, what several passages imply, that while
he was to a certain extent fond of astronomical study (as
to his capacity for which he clearly does injustice to himself
in the *House of Fame*), his good sense and his piety alike
revolted against extravagant astrological speculations.   He
certainly does not wish to go as far as the honest carpenter in the *Miller's Tale*, who glories in his incredulity
of aught besides his *credo*, and who yet is afterwards be-
fooled by the very impostor of whose astrological pursuits
he had reprehended the impiety.   " Men," he says, " should

know nothing of that which is private to God. Yea, blessed be alway a simple man who knows nothing but only his belief." In his little work *On the Astrolabe* Chaucer speaks with calm reasonableness of superstitions in which his spirit has no faith, and pleads guilty to ignorance of the useless knowledge with which they are surrounded. But the other, and perhaps the chief value, to us of this treatise lies in the fact that of Chaucer in an intimate personal relation it contains the only picture in which it is impossible to suspect any false or exaggerated colouring. For here we have him writing to his "little Lewis" with fatherly satisfaction in the ability displayed by the boy "to learn sciences touching numbers and proportions," and telling how, after making a present to the child of "a sufficient astrolabe as for our own horizon, composed after the latitude of Oxford," he has further resolved to explain to him a certain number of conclusions connected with the purposes of the instrument. This he has made up his mind to do in a forcible as well as simple way; for he has shrewdly divined a secret, now and then overlooked by those who condense sciences for babes, that children need to be taught a few things not only clearly but fully—repetition being in more senses than one "the mother of studies:"—

Now will I pray meekly every discreet person that readeth or heareth this little treatise, to hold my rude inditing excused, and my superfluity of words, for two causes. The first cause is: that curious inditing and hard sentences are full heavy at once for such a child to learn. And the second cause is this: that truly it seems better to me to write unto a child twice a good sentence, than to forget it once.

Unluckily we know nothing further of Lewis—not even whether, as has been surmised, he died before he had been able to turn to lucrative account his calculating powers, after the fashion of his apocryphal brother Thomas or otherwise.

Though by the latter part of the year 1391 Chaucer had lost his Clerkship of the Works, certain payments (possibly of arrears) seem afterwards to have been made to him in connexion with the office. A very disagreeable incident of his tenure of it had been a double robbery from his person of official money, to the very serious extent of twenty pounds. The perpetrators of the crime were a notorious gang of highwaymen, by whom Chaucer was, in September, 1390, apparently on the same day, beset both at Westminster, and near to "the foul Oak" at Hatcham in Surrey. A few months afterwards he was discharged by writ from repayment of the loss to the Crown. His experiences during the three years following are unknown; but in 1394 (when things were fairly quiet in England) he was granted an annual pension of twenty pounds by the King. This pension, of which several subsequent notices occur, seems at times to have been paid tardily or in small instalments, and also to have been frequently anticipated by Chaucer in the shape of loans of small sums. Further evidence of his straits is to be found in his having, in the year 1398, obtained letters of protection against arrest, making him safe for two years. The grant of a tun of wine in October of the same year is the last favour known to have been extended to Chaucer by King Richard II. Probably no English sovereign has been more diversely estimated, both by his contemporaries and by posterity, than this ill-fated prince, in the records of whose career many passages betokening high spirit strangely contrast with the impotence of its close. It will at least be remembered in his favour that he was a patron of the arts;

and that after Froissart had been present at his christen-
ing, he received, when on the threshold of manhood, the
homage of Gower, and on the eve of his downfall showed
most seasonable kindness to a poet far greater than either
of these.   It seems scarcely justifiable to assign to any
particular point of time the *Ballade sent to King Richard*
by Chaucer ; but its manifest intention was to apprise the
king of the poet's sympathy with his struggle against the
opponents of the royal policy, which was a thoroughly
autocratical one.   Considering the nature of the relations
between the pair, nothing could be more unlikely than
that Chaucer should have taken upon himself to exhort his
sovereign and patron to steadfastness of political conduct.
And in truth, though the loyal tone of this address is (as
already observed) unmistakeable enough, there is little
difficulty in accounting for the mixture of commonplace
reflexions and of admonitions to the king, to persist in a
spirited domestic policy.   He is to

> Dread God, do law, love truth and worthiness,

and wed his people—not himself—"again to steadfastness."
However, even a quasi-political poem of this description,
whatever element of implied flattery it may contain, offers
pleasanter reading than those least attractive of all occasional poems, of which the burden is a cry for money.
The *Envoy to Scogan* has been diversely dated, and diversely interpreted.   The reference in these lines to a
deluge of pestilence, clearly means, not a pestilence produced by heavy rains, but heavy rains which might be
expected to produce a pestilence.   The primary purpose
of the epistle admits of no doubt, though it is only revealed
in the postscript.   After bantering his friend on account
of his faint-heartedness in love—

Because thy lady saw not thy distress,
Therefore thou gavest her up at Michaelmas—

Chaucer ends by entreating him to further his claims upon
the royal munificence. Of this friend, Henry Scogan,
a tradition repeated by Ben Jonson averred that he
was a fine gentleman and Master of Arts of Henry IV.'s
time, who was regarded and rewarded for his Court
"disguisings" and "writings in ballad-royal." He is
therefore appropriately apostrophised by Chaucer as
kneeling

—— at the streamës head
Of grace, of all honoúr and worthiness,

and reminded that his friend is at the other end of the
current. The weariness of tone, natural under the circumstances, obscures whatever humour the poem possesses.
    Very possibly the lines to Scogan were written not
before, but immediately after, the accession of Henry IV.
In that case they belong to about the same date as the
wellknown and very plainspoken *Complaint of Chaucer to
his Purse*, addressed by him to the new Sovereign without
loss of time, if not indeed, as it would be hardly un-
charitable to suppose, prepared beforehand. Even in this
Complaint (the term was a technical one for an elegiac
piece, and was so used by Spenser) there is a certain frank
geniality of tone, the natural accompaniment of an easy
conscience, which goes some way to redeem the nature
of the subject. Still, the theme remains one which
only an exceptionally skilful treatment can make sufficiently pathetic or perfectly comic. The lines had the
desired effect; for within four days after his accession
—*i. e.* on October 3rd, 1399—the "conqueror of Brut's
Albion," otherwise King Henry IV., doubled Chaucer's

pension of twenty marks, so that, continuing as he did to enjoy the annuity of twenty pounds granted him by King Richard, he was now once more in comfortable circumstances. The best proof of these lies in the fact that very speedily—on Christmas Eve, 1399—Chaucer, probably in a rather sanguine mood, covenanted for the lease for fifty-three years of a house in the garden of the chapel of St. Mary at Westminster. And here, in comfort and in peace, as there seems every reason to believe, he died before another year, and with it the century, had quite run out—on October 25th, 1400.

Our fancy may readily picture to itself the last days of Geoffrey Chaucer, and the ray of autumn sunshine which gilded his reverend head before it was bowed in death. His old patron's more fortunate son, whose earlier chivalrous days we are apt to overlook in thinking of him as a politic king and the sagacious founder of a dynasty, cannot have been indifferent to the welfare of a subject for whose needs he had provided with so prompt a liberality. In the vicinity of a throne the smiles of royalty are wont to be contagious—and probably many a courtier thought well to seek the company of one who, so far as we know, had never forfeited the goodwill of any patron or the attachment of any friend. We may, too, imagine him visited by associates who loved and honoured the poet as well as the man—by Gower, blind or nearly so, if tradition speak the truth, and who, having "long had sickness upon hand," seems unlike Chaucer to have been ministered to in his old age by a housewife whom he had taken to himself in contradiction of principles preached by both the poets; and by "Bukton," converted, perchance, by means of Chaucer's gift to him of the *Wife of Bath's Tale*, to a resolution of

perpetual bachelorhood, but otherwise, as Mr. Carlyle
would say, "dim to us." Besides these, if he was still
among the living, the philosophical Strode in his
Dominican habit, on a visit to London from one of his
monasteries; or—more probably—the youthful Lydgate, not
yet a Benedictine monk, but pausing, on his return from
his travels in divers lands, to sit awhile, as it were, at the
feet of the master in whose poetic example he took pride;
the courtly Scogan; and Occleve, already learned, who
was to cherish the memory of Chaucer's outward features
as well as of his fruitful intellect :—all these may in his
closing days have gathered around their friend; and perhaps one or the other may have been present to close
the watchful eyes for ever.

But there was yet another company with which, in
these last years, and perhaps in these last days of his life,
Chaucer had intercourse, of which he can rarely have lost
sight, and which even in solitude he must have had
constantly with him. This company has since been
well known to generations and centuries of Englishmen.
Its members head that goodly procession of figures which
have been familiar to our fathers as livelong friends, which
are the same to us, and will be to our children after us—
the procession of the nation's favourites among the
characters created by our great dramatists and novelists,
the eternal types of human nature which nothing can
efface from our imagination. Or is there less reality about
the *Knight* in his short cassock and old-fashioned armour
and the *Wife of Bath* in hat and wimple, than—for
instance—about Uncle Toby and the Widow Wadman?
Can we not hear *Madame Eglantine* lisping her "Strat-
ford-atte-Bowe" French as if she were a personage in a
comedy by Congreve or Sheridan? Is not the *Summoner*

I

with his "fire-red cherubim's face" a worthy companion
for Lieutenant Bardolph himself? And have not the
humble *Parson* and his Brother the *Ploughman* that
irresistible pathos which Dickens could find in the simple
and the poor? All these figures, with those of their
fellow-pilgrims, are to us living men and women; and
in their midst the poet who created them lives, as he
has painted himself among the company, not less faithfully than Occleve depicted him from memory after death.

How long Chaucer had been engaged upon the *Canterbury Tales* it is impossible to decide. No process is more
hazardous than that of distributing a poet's works among
the several periods of his life according to divisions of
species—placing his tragedies or serious stories in one
season, his comedies or lighter tales in another, and so
forth. Chaucer no more admits of such treatment than
Shakspere, nor because there happens to be in his case
little actual evidence by which to control or contradict it,
are we justified in subjecting him to it. All we know
is that he left his great work a fragment, and that we
have no mention in any of his other poems of more than
three of the *Tales*—two, as already noticed, being mentioned in the Prologue to the Legend of Good Women,
written at a time when they had perhaps not yet assumed
the form in which they are preserved, while to the third
(the *Wife of Bath*) reference is made in the *Envoi to
Bukton*, the date of which is quite uncertain. At the
same time, the labour which was expended upon the *Canterbury Tales* by their author manifestly obliges us to
conclude that their composition occupied several years,
with inevitable interruptions; while the gaiety and brightness of many of the stories, and the exuberant humour
and exquisite pathos of others, as well as the masterly

effectiveness of the *Prologue,* make it almost certain
that these parts of the work were written when Chaucer
was not only capable of doing his best, but also in a
situation which admitted of his doing it. The supposition
is therefore a very probable one, that the main period of
their composition may have extended over the last eleven
or twelve years of his life, and have begun about the
time when ·he was again placed above want by his
appointment to the Clerkship of the Royal Works.

Again, it is virtually certain that the poem of the
Canterbury Tales was left in an unfinished and partially
unconnected condition, and it is altogether uncertain
whether Chaucer had finally determined upon maintaining
or modifying the scheme originally indicated by him in
the *Prologue.* There can accordingly be no necessity for
working out a scheme into which everything that he has
left belonging to the *Canterbury Tales* may most easily
and appropriately fit. Yet the labour is by no means
lost of such inquiries as those which have with singular
zeal been prosecuted concerning the several problems
that have to be solved before such a scheme can be completed. Without a review of the evidence it would however be preposterous to pronounce on the proper answer
to be given to the questions: what were the number of
tales and that of tellers ultimately designed by Chaucer;
what was the order in which he intended the *Tales* actually
written by him to stand; and what was the plan of the
journey of his pilgrims, as to the localities of its stages
and as to the time occupied by it—whether one day for
the fifty-six miles from London to Canterbury (which is
by no means impossible), or two days (which seems more
likely), or four. The route of the pilgrimage must have
been one in parts of which it is pleasant even now to

dally, when the sweet spring flowers are in bloom which
Mr. Boughton has painted for lovers of the poetry of
English landscape.

There are one or two other points which should not
be overlooked in considering the *Canterbury Tales* as a
whole. It has sometimes been assumed as a matter of
course that the plan of the work was borrowed from
Boccaccio. If this means that Chaucer owed to the
Decamerone the idea of including a number of stories
in the framework of a single narrative, it implies too
much. For this notion, a familiar one in the East, had
long been known to Western Europe by the numerous
versions of the terribly ingenious story of the *Seven
Wise Masters* (in the progress of which the unexpected
never happens), as well as by similar collections of the
same kind. And the special connexion of this device
with a company of pilgrims might, as has been well
remarked, have been suggested to Chaucer by an English
book certainly within his ken, the *Vision concerning Piers
Plowman,* where in the "fair field full of folk" are
assembled among others "pilgrims and palmers who went
forth on their way" to St. James of Compostella and to
saints at Rome "*with many wise tales*"—("and had leave
to lie all their life after"). But even had Chaucer owed
the idea of his plan to Boccaccio, he would not thereby
have incurred a heavy debt to the Italian novelist.
There is nothing really dramatic in the schemes of the
Decamerone, or of the numerous imitations which it called
forth, from the French *Heptaméron* and the Neapolitan
Pentamerone down to the German *Phantasus.* It is
unnecessary to come nearer to our own times; for the
author of the *Earthly Paradise* follows Chaucer in en-
deavouring at least to give a framework of real action

to his collection of poetic tales. There is no organic
connexion between the powerful narrative of the Plague
opening Boccaccio's book, and the stories chiefly of love
and its adventures which follow ; all that Boccaccio did
was to preface an interesting series of tales by a more interesting chapter of history, and then to bind the tales themselves together lightly and naturally in days, like rows of
pearls in a collar. But while in the *Decamerone* the framework in its relation to the stories is of little or no significance, in the *Canterbury Tales* it forms one of the most
valuable organic elements in the whole work. One test of
the distinction is this : what reader of the *Decamerone*
connects any of the novels composing it with the personality of the particular narrator, or even cares to
remember the grouping of the stories as illustrations of
fortunate or unfortunate, adventurous or illicit, passion ?
The charm of Boccaccio's book, apart from the independent merits of the Introduction, lies in the admirable
skill and unflagging vivacity with which the "novels"
themselves are told. The scheme of the *Canterbury Tales,*
on the other hand, possesses some genuinely dramatic
elements. If the entire form, at all events in its extant
condition, can scarcely be said to have a plot, it at least
has an *exposition* unsurpassed by that of any comedy,
ancient or modern ; it has the possibility of a growth of
action and interest ; and (which is of far more importance, it has a variety of characters which mutually
both relieve and supplement one another. With how
sure an instinct, by the way, Chaucer has anticipated that
unwritten law of the modern drama according to which
low comedy characters always appear in couples ! Thus
the *Miller* and the *Reeve* are a noble pair running in
parallel lines, though in contrary directions ; so are the

Cook and the *Manciple,* and again and more especially
the *Friar* and the *Summoner.* Thus at least the germ of
a comedy exists in the plan of the *Canterbury Tales.*
No comedy could be formed out of the mere circumstance
of a company of ladies and gentlemen sitting down in
a country-house to tell an unlimited number of stories
on a succession of topics; but a comedy could be written
with the purpose of showing how a wide variety of
national types will present themselves, when brought
into mutual contact by an occasion peculiarly fitted
to call forth their individual rather than their common
characteristics.

For not only are we at the opening of the *Canterbury
Tales* placed in the very heart and centre of English life;
but the poet contrives to find for what may be called his
action a background, which seems of itself to suggest the
most serious emotions and the most humorous associations.
And this without anything grotesque in the collocation,
such as is involved in the notion of men telling anecdotes
at a funeral, or forgetting a pestilence over love-stories.
Chaucer's *dramatis personæ* are a company of pilgrims,
whom at first we find assembled in a hostelry in Southwark, and whom we afterwards accompany on their journey
to Canterbury. The hostelry is that *Tabard* inn which,
though it changed its name, and no doubt much of its
actual structure, long remained both in its general appearance, and perhaps in part of its actual self, a genuine relic
of mediæval London. There, till within a very few years
from the present date, might still be had a draught of that
London ale of which Chaucer's *Cook* was so thorough a
connoisseur; and there within the big courtyard, surrounded
by a gallery very probably a copy of its predecessor, was
ample room for

—— well nine and twenty in a company
Of sundry folk,

with their horses and travelling gear sufficient for a ride
to Canterbury. The goal of this ride has its religious, its
national, one might even say its political aspect ; but the
journey itself has an importance of its own. A journey
is generally one of the best of opportunities for bringing
out the distinctive points in the characters of travellers ;
and we are accustomed to say that no two men can long
travel in one another's company unless their friendship is
equal to the severest of tests. At home men live mostly
among colleagues and comrades ; on a journey they are
placed in continual contrast with men of different pursuits
and different habits of life. The shipman away from his
ship, the monk away from his cloister, the scholar away
from his books, become interesting instead of remaining
commonplace, because the contrasts become marked which
exist between them. Moreover, men undertake journeys
for divers purposes, and a pilgrimage in Chaucer's day
united a motley group of chance companions in search of
different ends at the same goal. One goes to pray, the
other seeks profit, the third distraction, the fourth pleasure.
To some the road is everything ; to others, its terminus.
All this vanity lay in the mere choice of Chaucer's framework ; there was accordingly something of genius in the
thought itself ; and even an inferior workmanship could
hardly have left a description of a Canterbury pilgrimage
unproductive of a wide variety of dramatic effects.

   But Chaucer's workmanship was as admirable as his
selection of his framework was felicitous. He has executed
only part of his scheme, according to which each pilgrim
was to tell two tales both going and coming, and the
best narrator, the laureate of this merry company, was

to be rewarded by a supper at the common expense
on their return to their starting-place. Thus the design
was, not merely to string together a number of poetical
tales by an easy thread, but to give a real unity and completeness to the whole poem. All the tales told by all the
pilgrims were to be connected together by links; the
reader was to take an interest in the movement and
progress of the journey to and fro ; and the poem was to
have a middle as well as a beginning and an end :—the
beginning being the inimitable *Prologue* as it now stands ;
the middle the history of the pilgrims' doings at Canterbury ; and the close their return and farewell celebration
at the Tabard inn. Though Chaucer carried out only
about a fourth part of this plan, yet we can see, as clearly
as if the whole poem lay before us in a completed form,
that its most salient feature was intended to lie in the
variety of its characters.

Each of these characters is distinctly marked out in
itself, while at the same time it is designed as the type
of a class. This very obvious criticism of course most
readily admits of being illustrated by the *Prologue*—a
gallery of *genre*-portraits which many master-hands have
essayed to reproduce with pen or with pencil. Indeed
one lover of Chaucer sought to do so with both—poor
gifted Blake, whose descriptive text of his picture of
the Canterbury Pilgrims Charles Lamb, with the loving
exaggeration in which he was at times fond of indulging,
pronounced the finest criticism on Chaucer's poem he
had ever read. But it should be likewise noticed that
the character of each pilgrim is kept up through the
poem, both incidentally in the connecting passages between tale and tale, and in the manner in which the
tales themselves are introduced and told. The con-

necting passages are full of dramatic vivacity; in these
the *Host*, Master Harry Bailly, acts as a most efficient
choragus, but the other pilgrims are not silent, and in the
Manciple's Prologue, the *Cook* enacts a bit of downright
farce for the amusement of the company and of stray
inhabitants of " Bob-up-and-down." He is, however,
homœopathically cured of the effects of his drunkenness,
so that the *Host* feels justified in offering up a thanks-
giving to Bacchus for his powers of conciliation. The
Man of Law's Prologue is an argument ; the *Wife of Bath's*
the ceaseless clatter of an indomitable tongue. The
sturdy *Franklin* corrects himself when deviating into
circumlocution :—

> Till that the brightë sun had lost his hue,
> For th' hórizon had reft the sun of light,
> (This is as much to say as : it was night).

The *Miller* " tells his churlish tale in his manner," of
which manner the less said the better ; while in the *Reeve's
Tale*, Chaucer even, after the manner of a comic dramatist,
gives his Northern undergraduate a vulgar ungrammatical
phraseology, probably designedly, since the poet was himself a " Southern man." The *Pardoner* is exuberant in
his sample-eloquence ; the *Doctor of Physic* is gravely and
sententiously moral—

> —— a proper man,
> And like a prelate, by Saint Runyan,

says the *Host*. Most sustained of all, though he tells no
tale, is, from the nature of the case, the character of Harry
Bailly, the host of the Tabard, himself—who, whatever
resemblance he may bear to his actual original, is the ances-
tor of a long line of descendants, including mine Host of
the Garter in the *Merry Wives of Windsor*. He is a

thorough worldling, to whom anything smacking of the pre-
cisian in morals is as offensive as anything of a Romantic
tone in literature; he smells a Lollard without fail, and
turns up his nose at an old-fashioned ballad or a string
of tragic instances as out of date or tedious.   In short, he
speaks his mind and that of other more timid people at
the same time, and is one of those sinners whom everybody
both likes and respects.   " I advise," says the *Pardoner,*
with polite impudence (when inviting the company to
become purchasers of the holy wares which he has for
sale), that

> —— our host, he shall begin,
> For he is most envelopèd in sin.

He is thus both an admirable picture in himself, and an
admirable foil to those characters which are most unlike
him—above all to the *Parson* and the *Clerk of Oxford,*
the representatives of religion and learning.

As to the *Tales* themselves, Chaucer beyond a doubt
meant their style and tone to be above all things *popular.*
This is one of the causes accounting for the favour shown
to the work,—a favour attested, so far as earlier times are
concerned, by the vast number of manuscripts existing of
it.   The *Host* is, so to speak, charged with the constant
injunction of this cardinal principle of popularity as to
both theme and style.   "Tell us," he coolly demands of
the most learned and sedate of all his fellow-travellers,

> —— some merry thing of ádventures;
> Your termës, your coloúrs, and your figúres,
> Keep them in store, till so be ye indite
> High style, as when that men to kingës write;
> Speak ye so plain at this time, we you pray,
> That we may understandë that ye say.

And the *Clerk* follows the spirit of the injunction both

by omitting, as impertinent, a proeme in which his
original, Petrarch, gives a great deal of valuable, but not
in its connexion interesting, geographical information,
and by adding a facetious moral to what he calls the
"unrestful matter" of his story.   Even the *Squire*,
though, after the manner of young men, far more than
his elders addicted to the grand style, and accordingly
specially praised for his eloquence by the simple *Franklin*,
prefers to reduce to its plain meaning the courtly speech of
the Knight of the Brazen Steed.   In connexion with what
was said above, it is observable that each of the *Tales* in subject suits its narrator.   Not by chance is the all-but-
Quixotic romance of *Palamon and Arcite*, taken by Chaucer
from Boccaccio's *Teseide*, related by the *Knight;* not by
chance does the *Clerk*, following Petrarch's Latin version
of a story related by the same author, tell the even more
improbable, but, in the plainness of its moral, infinitely
more fructuous tale of patient Griseldis.   How well the
Second Nun is fitted with a legend which carries us back a
few centuries into the atmosphere of Hrosvitha's comedies,
and suggests with the utmost verisimilitude the nature of
a nun's lucubrations on the subject of marriage.   It is
impossible to go through the whole list of the *Tales ;* but
all may be truly said to be in keeping with the characters
and manners (often equally indifferent) of their tellers—
down to that of the *Nun's Priest*, which, brimful of
humour as it is, has just the mild naughtiness about it
which comes so *drolly from a spiritual director in his
worldlier hour.

Not a single one of these *Tales* can with any show of
reason be ascribed to Chaucer's own invention.   French
literature—chiefly though not solely that of *fabliaux*—
doubtless supplied the larger share of his materials ; but

that here also his debts to Italian literature, and to
Boccaccio in particular, are considerable, seems hardly to
admit of denial.   But while Chaucer freely borrowed from
foreign models, he had long passed beyond the stage of
translating without assimilating.   It would be rash to
assume that where he altered he invariably improved.   His
was not the unerring eye which, like Shakspere's in his
dramatic transfusions of Plutarch, missed no particle of the
gold mingled with the baser metal, but rejected the dross
with sovereign certainty.   In dealing with Italian originals
more especially, he sometimes altered for the worse, and
sometimes for the better ; but he was never a mere slavish
translator.   So in the *Knight's Tale* he may be held in
some points to have deviated disadvantageously from his
original ; but, on the other hand, in the *Clerk's Tale*, he
inserts a passage on the fidelity of women, and another on
the instability of the multitude, besides adding a touch of
nature irresistibly pathetic in the exclamation of the
faithful wife, tried beyond her power of concealing the
emotion within her :

> O gracious God ! how gentle and how kind
> Ye seeméd by your speech and your viságe
> The day that makéd was our marriáge.

So also in the *Man of Law's Tale*, which is taken from
the French, he increases the vivacity of the narrative by
a considerable number of apostrophes in his own favourite
manner, besides pleasing the general reader by divers
general reflexions of his own inditing. Almost necessarily,
the literary form and the self-consistency of his originals lose
under such treatment.   But his dramatic sense, on which
perhaps his commentators have not always sufficiently
dwelt, is rarely, if ever, at fault.   Two illustrations of
this gift in Chaucer must suffice, which shall be chosen in

two quarters where he has worked with materials of the
most widely different kind. Many readers must have
compared with Dante's original (in canto xxxiii. of the
Inferno) Chaucer's version in the *Monk's Tale* of the
story of Ugolino. Chaucer, while he necessarily omits
the ghastly introduction, expands the pathetic picture of
the sufferings of the father and his sons in their dungeon,
and closes, far more briefly and effectively than Dante,
with a touch of the most refined pathos :—

DE HUGILINO COMITE PISÆ.

Of Hugolin of Pisa the languór
There may no tonguë tellë for pitý.
But little out of Pisa stands a tower,
In whichë tower in prison put was he ;
And with him be his little children three.
The eldest scarcely five years was of age ;
Alas! fortúne ! it was great cruelty
Such birds as these to put in such a cage.

Condemned he was to die in that prisón,
For Royer, which that bishop was of Pise,
Had on him made a false suggestióñ,
Through which the people gan on him arise,
And put him in prisón in such a wise,
As ye have heard, and meat and drink he had
So little that it hardly might suffice,
And therewithal it was full poor and bad.

And on a day befell that in that hour
When that his meat was wont to be y-brought,
The gaoler shut the doorës of that tower.
IIe heard it well, although he saw it not ;
And in his heart anon there fell a thought
That they his death by hunger did devise.
"Alas ! " quoth he, " alas ! that I was wrought ! "
Therewith the tearës fellë from his eyes.

His youngest son, that three years was of age,
Unto him said : "Father, why do ye weep?
When will the gaoler bring us our pottáge?
Is there no morsel bread that ye do keep?
I am so hungry that I cannot sleep.
Now wouldë God that I might sleep for ever!
Then should not hunger in my belly creep.
There is no thing save bread that I would liever."

Thus day by day this child began to cry,
Till in his father's lap adown he lay,
And saidë: "Farewell, father, I must die!"
And kissed his father, and died the samë day.
The woeful father saw that dead he lay,
And his two arms for woe began to bite,
And said : "Fortune, alas and well-away !
For all my woe I blame thy treacherous spite."

His children weened that it for hunger was,
That he his armës gnawed, and not for woe.
And saidë: "Father, do not so, alas !
But rather eat the flesh upon us two.
Our flesh thou gavest us, our flesh thou take us fro,
And eat enough." Right thus they to him cried ;
And after that, within a day or two,
They laid them in his lap adown and died.

The father in despair likewise died of hunger ; and such
was the end of the mighty Earl of Pisa, whose tragedy
whosoever desires to hear at greater length may read it
as told by the great poet of Italy hight Dante.

The other instance is that of *The Pardoner's Tale*, which
would appear to have been based on a *fabliau* now lost,
though the substance of it is preserved in an Italian novel,
and in one or two other versions. For the purpose of
noticing how Chaucer arranges as well as tells a story, the
following attempt at a condensed prose rendering of his
narrative may be acceptable :—

Once upon a time in Flanders there was a company of
young men, who gave themselves up to every kind of
dissipation and debauchery—haunting the taverns where
dancing and dicing continues day and night, eating and
drinking, and serving the devil in his own temple by their
outrageous life of luxury. It was horrible to hear their
oaths, how they tore to pieces our blessed Lord's body, as
if they thought the Jews had not rent Him enough ; and
each laughed at the sin of the others, and all were alike
immersed in gluttony and wantonness.

And so one morning it befel that three of these rioters
were sitting over their drink in a tavern, long before
the bell had rung for nine o'clock prayers. And as they
sat, they heard a bell clinking before a corpse that was being
carried to the grave. So one of them bade his servant-lad
go and ask what was the name of the dead man ; but
the boy said that he knew it already, and that it was the
name of an old companion of his master's. As he had been
sitting drunk on a bench, there had come a privy thief,
whom men called Death, and who slew all the people in
this country ; and he had smitten the drunken man's heart
in two with his spear, and had then gone on his way
without any more words. This Death had slain a thousand
during the present pestilence ; and the boy thought it
worth warning his master to beware of such an adversary,
and to be ready to meet him at any time. "So my mother
taught me ; I say no more." "Marry," said the keeper
of the tavern ; "the child tells the truth : this Death has
slain all the inhabitants of a great village not far from here;
I think that there must be the place where he dwells."
Then the rioter swore with some of his big oaths that he
at least was not afraid of this Death, and that he would
seek him out wherever he dwelt. And at his instance his

two boon-companions joined with him in a vow that before
nightfall they would slay the false traitor Death, who was
the slayer of so many ; and the vow they swore was one of
closest fellowship between them—to live and die for one
another as if they had been brethren born. And so they
went forth in their drunken fury towards the village of
which the taverner had spoken, with terrible execrations
on their lips that "Death should be dead, if they might
catch him."

They had not gone quite half a mile when at a stile
between two fields they came upon a poor old man, who
meekly greeted them with a "God save you, sirs." But
the proudest of the three rioters answered him roughly,
asking him why he kept himself all wrapped up except his
face, and how so old a fellow as he had managed to keep
alive so long? And the old man looked him straight in
the face and replied, "Because in no town or village,
though I journey as far as the Indies, can I find a man
willing to exchange his youth for my age ; and therefore I
must keep it so long as God wills it so. Death, alas !
will not have my life, and so I wander about like a rest-
less fugitive, and early and late I knock on the ground,
which is my mother's gate, with my staff, and say, 'Dear
mother, let me in ! behold how I waste away ! Alas !
when shall my bones be at rest? Mother, gladly will I
give you my chest containing all my worldly gear in return for a shroud to wrap me in.' But she refuses me that
grace, and that is why my face is pale and withered. But
you, sirs, are uncourteous to speak rudely to an inoffensive
old man, when Holy Writ bids you reverence grey hairs.
Therefore, never again give offence to an old man, if you
wish men to be courteous to you in your age, should you
live so long. And so God be with you ; I must go whither

I have to go." But the second rioter prevented him, and
swore he should not depart so lightly. "Thou spakest
just now of that traitor Death, who slays all our friends
in this country. As thou art his spy, hear me swear that,
unless thou tellest where he is, thou shalt die; for thou
art in his plot to slay us young men, thou false thief!"
Then the old man told them that if they were so desirous
of finding Death, they had but to turn up a winding path
to which he pointed, and there they would find him they
sought in a grove under an oak-tree, where the old man
had just left him; "he will not try to hide himself for all
your boasting. And so may God the Redeemer save you
and amend you!" And when he had spoken, all the three
rioters ran till they came to the tree. But what they found
there was a treasure of golden florins—nearly seven bushels
of them as they thought. Then they no longer sought after
Death, but sat down all three by the shining gold. And
the youngest of them spoke first, and declared that Fortune
had given this treasure to them, so that they might spend
the rest of their lives in mirth and jollity. The question
was how to take this money—which clearly belonged to
some one else—safely to the house of one of the three
companions. It must be done by night; so let them draw
lots, and let him on whom the lot fell run to the town to
fetch bread and wine, while the other two guarded the
treasure carefully till the night came, when they might
agree whither to transport it.

The lot fell on the youngest, who forthwith went his
way to the town. Then one of those who remained with
the treasure said to the other: "Thou knowest well that
thou art my sworn brother, and I will tell thee something
to thy advantage. Our companion is gone, and here is a
great quantity of gold to be divided among us three. But

K

say, if I could manage so that the gold is divided between us two, should I not do thee a friend's turn?" And when the other failed to understand him, he made him promise secrecy and disclosed his plan. "Two are stronger than one. When he sits down, arise as if thou wouldest sport with him; and while thou art struggling with him as in play, I will rive him through both his sides; and look thou do the same with thy dagger. After which, my dear friend, we will divide all the gold between you and me, and then we may satisfy all our desires and play at dice to our hearts' content."

Meanwhile the youngest rioter, as he went up to the town, revolved in his heart the beauty of the bright new florins, and said unto himself: "If only I could have all this gold to myself alone, there is no man on earth who would live so merrily as I." And at last the Devil put it into his relentless heart to buy poison, in order with it to kill his two companions. And straightway he went on into the town to an apothecary, and besought him to sell him some poison for destroying some rats which infested his house and a polecat which, he said, had made away with his capons. And the apothecary said : "Thou shalt have something of which (so may God save my soul!) no creature in all the world could swallow a single grain without losing his life thereby—and that in less time than thou wouldest take to walk a mile in." So the miscreant shut up this poison in a box, and then he went into the next street and borrowed three large bottles, into two of which he poured his poison, while the third he kept clean to hold drink for himself; for he meant to work hard all the night to carry away the gold. So he filled his three bottles with wine, and then went back to his companions under the tree.

What need to make a long discourse of what followed?
As they had plotted their comrade's death, so they
slew him, and that at once. And when they had done
this, the one who had counselled the deed said, " Now let
us sit and drink and make merry, and then we will bury
his body." And it happened to him by chance to take
one of the bottles which contained the poison; and he
drank, and gave drink of it to his fellow; and thus they
both speedily died.

The plot of this story is, as observed, not Chaucer's.
But how carefully, how artistically the narrative is elabo-
rated, incident by incident, and point by point! How
well every effort is prepared, and how well every turn of
the story is explained! Nothing is superfluous, but
everything is arranged with care, down to the circumstances of the bottles being bought, for safety's sake, in
the next street to the apothecary's, and of two out of
three bottles being filled with poison, which is at once a
proceeding natural in itself, and increases the chances
against the two rioters when they are left to choose for
themselves. This it is to be a good story-teller. But of a
different order is the change introduced by Chaucer into
his original, where the old hermit—who, of course, is
Death himself—is fleeing from Death. Chaucer's Old
Man is *seeking* Death, but seeking him in vain—like
the Wandering Jew of the legend. This it is to be a
poet.

Of course it is always necessary to be cautious before
asserting any apparent addition of Chaucer's to be his own
invention. Thus, in the *Merchant's Tale*, the very naughty
plot of which is anything but original, it is impossible to
say whether such is the case with the humorous competi-

tion of advice between Justinus and Placebo,[1] or with the
fantastic machinery in which Pluto and Proserpine anti-
cipate the part played by Oberon and Titania in *A Mid-
summer Night's Dream.* On the other hand, Chaucer is
capable of using goods manifestly borrowed or stolen for a
purpose never intended in their original employment.
Puck himself must have guided the audacious hand which
could turn over the leaves of so respected a Father of the
Church as St. Jerome, in order to derive from his treatise
On Perpetual Virginity materials for the discourse on
matrimony delivered, with illustrations essentially her own,
by the *Wife of Bath.*

Two only among these *Tales* are in prose—a vehicle of
expression, on the whole, strange to the polite literature
of the pre-Renascence ages—but not both for the same
reason. The first of these *Tales* is told by the poet himself, after a stop has been unceremoniously put upon his
recital of the *Ballad of Sir Thopas* by the Host. The
ballad itself is a fragment of straightforward burlesque,
which shows that in both the manner and the metre [2] of
ancient romances, literary criticism could even in Chaucer's
days find its opportunities for satire, though it is going
rather far to see in *Sir Thopas* a predecessor of *Don
Quixote.* The *Tale of Meliboeus* is probably an English version of a French translation of Albert of Brescia's famous
Book of Consolation and Counsel, which comprehends in a
slight narrative framework a long discussion between the
unfortunate Meliboeus, whom the wrongs and sufferings

---

[1] "Placebo" seems to have been a current term to express the
character or the ways of "the too deferential man." "Flatterers
be the Devil's chaplains, that sing aye *Placebo.*"—*Parson's Tale.*

[2] Dunbar's burlesque ballad of *Sir Thomas Norray* is in the
same stanza.

inflicted upon him and his have brought to the verge of
despair, and his wise helpmate, Dame Prudence.　By
means of a long argumentation propped up by quotations
(not invariably assigned with conscientious accuracy to
their actual source) from " The Book," Seneca, " Tullius,"
and other authors, she at last persuades him not only to
reconcile himself to his enemies, but to forgive them, even
as he hopes to be forgiven.　And thus the Tale well
bears out the truth impressed upon Meliboeus by the
following ingeniously combined quotation :—

And there said once a clerk in two verses : What is better
than gold ? Jasper. And what is better than jasper ? Wisdom. And what is better than wisdom ? Woman. And what
is better than woman ? No thing.

Certainly, Chaucer gave proof of consummate tact and taste,
as well as of an unaffected personal modesty, in assigning
to himself as one of the company of pilgrims, instead of
a tale bringing him into competition with the creatures of
his own invention, after his mocking ballad has served its
turn, nothing more ambitious than a version of a popular
discourse—half narrative, half homily—in prose.　But a
question of far greater difficulty and moment arises with
regard to the other prose piece included among the *Canterbury Tales*.　Of these the so-called *Parson's Tale* is the
last in order of succession.　Is it to be looked upon as an
integral part of the collection ; and, if so, what general and
what personal significance should be attached to it？

As it stands, the long tractate or sermon (partly
adapted from a popular French religious manual), which
bears the name of the *Parson's Tale*, is, if not unfinished,
at least internally incomplete.　It lacks symmetry, and
fails entirely to make good the argument or scheme
of divisions with which the sermon begins, as conscien-

tiously as one of Barrow's.   Accordingly, an attempt has
been made to show that what we have is something different from the "meditation" which Chaucer originally put
into his *Parson's* mouth.   But, while we may stand in
respectful awe of the German daring which, whether the
matter in hand be a few pages of Chaucer, a Book of
Homer, or a chapter of the Old Testament, is fully prepared to show which parts of each are mutilated, which
interpolated, and which transposed, we may safely content
ourselves, in the present instance, with considering the
preliminary question.   *A priori*, is there sufficient reason
for supposing any transpositions, interpolations, and muti-
lations to have been introduced into the *Parson's Tale ?*
The question is full of interest; for while, on the one
hand, the character of the *Parson* in the *Prologue* has
been frequently interpreted as evidence of sympathy on
Chaucer's part with Wycliffism, on the other hand, the
Parson's Tale, in its extant form, goes far to disprove the
supposition that its author was a Wycliffite.

This, then, seems the appropriate place for briefly reviewing the vexed question—*Was Chaucer a Wycliffite ?*
Apart from the character of the *Parson* and from the
Parson's Tale, what is the nature of our evidence on the
subject ?   In the first place, nothing could be clearer than
that Chaucer was a very free-spoken critic of the life of
the clergy—more especially of the Regular clergy—of his
times.   In this character he comes before us from his
translation of the *Roman de la Rose* to the *Parson's Tale*
itself, where he inveighs with significant earnestness
against self-indulgence on the part of those who are Religious, or have "entered into Orders, as sub-deacon, or
deacon, or priest, or hospitallers."   In the *Canterbury
Tales*, above all, his attacks upon the Friars run nearly

the whole gamut of satire, stopping short perhaps before
the note of high moral indignation. Moreover, as has
been seen, his long connexion with John of Gaunt is a
well-established fact ; and it has thence been concluded
that Chaucer fully shared the opinions and tendencies represented by his patron. In the supposition that Chaucer
approved of the countenance for a long time shown by
John of Gaunt to Wyclif there is nothing improbable ;
neither, however, is there anything improbable in this
other supposition, that, when the Duke of Lancaster openly
washed his hands of the heretical tenets to the utterance of
which Wyclif had advanced, Chaucer, together with the
large majority of Englishmen, held with the politic duke
rather than with the still unflinching Reformer. So long
as Wyclif's movement consisted only of an opposition to
ecclesiastical pretensions on the one hand, and of an
attempt to revive religious sentiment on the other, half
the country or more was Wycliffite, and Chaucer no doubt
with the rest. But it would require positive evidence to
justify the belief that from this feeling Chaucer ever
passed to sympathy with *Lollardry,* in the vague but sufficiently intelligible sense attaching to that term in the latter
part of Richard the Second's reign. Richard II. himself,
whose patronage of Chaucer is certain, in the end attempted rigorously to suppress Lollardry ; and Henry
IV., the politic John of Gaunt's yet more politic son, to
whom Chaucer owed the prosperity enjoyed by him in the
last year of his life, became a persecutor almost as soon as
he became a king.

Though, then, from the whole tone of his mind, Chaucer
could not but sympathise with the opponents of ecclesiastical domination—though, as a man of free and critical
spirit, and of an inborn ability for penetrating beneath the

surface, he could not but find subjects for endless blame
and satire in the members of those Mendicant Orders in
whom his chief patron's academical ally had recognised
the most formidable obstacles to the spread of pure religion—yet all this would not justify us in regarding him
as personally a Wycliffite. Indeed, we might as well at
once borrow the phraseology of a recent respectable critic,
and set down Dan Chaucer as a Puritan ! The policy of
his patron tallied with the view which a fresh practical
mind such as Chaucer's would naturally be disposed to
take of the influence of monks and friars, or at least
of those monks and friars whose vices and foibles were
specially prominent in his eyes. There are various reasons
why men oppose established institutions in the season of
their decay; but a fourteenth century satirist of the
monks, or even of the clergy at large, was not necessarily
a Lollard, any more than a nineteenth century objector to
doctors' drugs is necessarily a homœopathist.

But, it is argued by some, Chaucer has not only assailed
the false ; he has likewise extolled the true. He has
painted both sides of the contrast. On the one side are
the Monk, the Friar, and the rest of their fellows ; on the
other is the *Poor Parson of a town*—a portrait, if not of
Wyclif himself, at all events of a Wycliffite priest ; and
in the *Tale* or sermon put in the Parson's mouth are
recognisable beneath the accumulations of interested editors
some of the characteristic marks of Wycliffism. Who is
not acquainted with the exquisite portrait in question ?—

> A good man was there of religión,
> And was a poorë Parson of a town.
> But rich he was of holy thought and work.
> He was also a learnèd man, a clerk
> That Christës Gospel truly wouldë preach ;
> And his parishioners devoutly teach.

Benign he was, and wondrous diligent,
And in adversity full patiént.
And such he was y-provèd oftë sithes.
Full loth he was to curse men for his tithes;
But rather would he givë, without doubt,
Unto his poor parishioners about
Of his off'ríng and eke of his substánce.
He could in little wealth have súffisance.
Wide was his parish, houses far asunder,
Yet failed he not for either rain or thunder
In sickness nor mischance to visit all
The furthest in his parish, great and small,
Upon his feet, and in his hand a staff.
This noble ensample to his sheep he gave,
That first he wrought, and afterwards he taught;
Out of the Gospel he those wordës caught,
And this figúre he added eke thereto,
That " if gold rustë, what shall iron do ? "
For if a priest be foul, on whom we trust,
No wonder is it if a layman rust;
And shame it is, if that a priest take keep,
A foul shepherd to see and a clean sheep;
Well ought a priest ensample for to give
By his cleannéss, how that his sheep should live.
He put not out his benefice on hire,
And left his sheep encumbered in the mire,
And ran to London unto Saintë Paul's,
To seek himself a chantery for souls,
Or maintenance with a brotherhood to hold;
But dwelt at home, and keptë well his fold,
So that the wolf ne'er made it to miscarry;
He was a shepherd and no mercenáry.
And though he holy were, and virtuous,
He was to sinful man not déspitous,
And of his speech nor difficult nor digne,
But in his teaching díscreet and benign.
For to draw folk to heaven by fairnéss,
By good ensample, this was his business:
But were there any person obstinate,
What so he were, of high or low estate,
Him would he sharply snub at once.   Than this

> A better priest, I trow, there nowhere is.
> He waited for no pomp and reverence,
> Nor made himself a spicèd consciénce ;
> But Christës lore and His Apostles' twelve
> He taught, but first he followed it himself.

The most striking features in this portrait are undoubtedly those which are characteristics of the good and
humble working clergyman of all times ; and some of
these, accordingly, Goldsmith could appropriately borrow
for his gentle poetic sketch of his parson-brother in " Sweet
Auburn." But there are likewise points in the sketch
which may be fairly described as specially distinctive of
Wyclif's Simple Priests—though, as should be pointed out,
these Priests could not themselves be designated parsons
of towns. Among the latter features are the specially
evangelical source of the *Parson's* learning and teaching ;
and his outward appearance—the wandering, staff in
hand, which was specially noted in an archiepiscopal
diatribe against these novel ministers of the people. Yet
it seems unnecessary to conclude anything beyond this :
that the feature which Chaucer desired above all to mark
and insist upon in his *Parson,* was the poverty and humility
which in him contrasted with the luxurious self-indulgence of the *Monk*, and the blatant insolence of the *Pardoner*. From this point of view it is obvious why the
Parson is made brother to the *Ploughman*. For, in drawing the latter, Chaucer cannot have forgotten that other
Ploughman whom Langland's poem had identified with
Him for whose sake Chaucer's poor workman laboured
for his poor neighbours, with the readiness always shown
by the best of his class. Nor need this recognition of the
dignity of the lowly surprise us in Chaucer, who had both
sense of justice and sense of humour enough not to flatter
one class at the expense of the rest, and who elsewhere

(in the *Manciple's Tale*) very forcibly puts the truth that
what in a great man is called a *coup d'état* is called by
a much simpler name in a humbler fellow-sinner.

But though, in the *Parson of a Town*, Chaucer may
not have wished to paint a Wycliffite priest—still less a
Lollard, under which designation so many varieties of
malcontents, in addition to the followers of Wyclif, were
popularly included—yet his eyes and ears were open;
and he knew well enough what the world and its children
are at all times apt to call those who are not ashamed of
their religion, as well as those who make too conscious a
profession of it. The world called them Lollards at the
close of the fourteenth century, and it called them Puri-
tans at the close of the sixteenth, and Methodists at
the close of the eighteenth. Doubtless the vintners and
the shipmen of Chaucer's day, the patrons and purveyors
of the playhouse in Ben Jonson's, the fox-hunting squires
and town wits of Cowper's, like their successors after
them, were not specially anxious to distinguish nicely between more or less abominable varieties of saintliness.
Hence, when Master Harry Bailly's tremendous oaths produce the gentlest of protests from the *Parson*, the jovial
Host incontinently "smells a Lollard in the wind," and
predicts (with a further flow of expletives) that there is a
sermon to follow. Whereupon the *Shipman* protests not
less characteristically :—

> "Nay, by my father's soul, that shall he not,"
> Saidë the Shipman, "here shall he not preach,
> He shall no gospel here explain or teach.
> We all believe in the great God," quoth he ;
> "He wouldë sowë some difficulty,
> Or springë cockle in our cleanë corn." [1]

---

[1] The nickname Lollards was erroneously derived from *lolia* (tares).

After each of the pilgrims except the *Parson* has told a
tale (so that obviously Chaucer designed one of the divisions of his work to close with the *Parson's*), he is again
called upon by the *Host*.   Hereupon appealing to the undoubtedly evangelical and, it might without straining be
said, Wycliffite authority of Timothy, he promises as his
contribution a " merry tale in prose," which proves to consist of a moral discourse.   In its extant form the *Parson's
Tale* contains, by the side of much that might suitably have
come from a Wycliffite teacher, much of a directly opposite
nature.   For not only is the necessity of certain sacra-
mental usages to which Wyclif strongly objected insisted
upon, but the spoliation of Church property is unctuously
inveighed against as a species of one of the cardinal sins.
No enquiry could satisfactorily establish how much of this
was taken over or introduced into the *Parson's Tale* by
Chaucer himself.   But one would fain at least claim for
him a passage in perfect harmony with the character drawn
of the *Parson* in the *Prologue*—a passage (already cited
in part in the opening section of the present essay) where
the poet advocates the cause of the poor in words which,
simple as they are, deserve to be quoted side by side with
that immortal character itself.   The concluding lines may
therefore be cited here :—

Think also that of the same seed of which churls spring, of
the same seed spring lords ; as well may the churl be saved as
the lord.   Wherefore I counsel thee, do just so with thy churl
as thou wouldest thy lord did with thee, if thou wert in his
plight.   A very sinful man is a churl as towards sin.   I counsel
thee certainly, thou lord, that thou work in such wise with thy
churls that they rather love thee than dread thee.   I know
well, where there is degree above degree, it is reasonable that
men should do their duty where it is due ; but of a certainty,
extortions, and despite of our underlings, are damnable.

In sum, the *Parson's Tale* cannot, any more than the
character of the *Parson* in the *Prologue*, be interpreted as
proving Chaucer to have been a Wycliffite.   But the one
as well as the other proves him to have perceived much of
what was noblest in the Wycliffite movement, and much
of what was ignoblest in the reception with which it met
at the hands of worldlings—before, with the aid of the
State, the Church finally succeeded in crushing it, to all
appearance, out of existence.

The *Parson's Tale* contains a few vigorous touches, in
addition to the fine passage quoted, which make it difficult to deny that Chaucer's hand was concerned in it.
The inconsistency between the religious learning ascribed
to the *Parson* and a passage in the *Tale*, where the author
leaves certain things to be settled by divines, will not be
held of much account.   The most probable conjecture
seems therefore to be that the discourse has come down to
us in a mutilated form.   This *may* be due to the *Tale*
having remained unfinished at the time of Chaucer's death :
in which case it would form last words of no unfitting
kind.   As for the actual last words of the *Canterbury
Tales*—the so-called *Prayer of Chaucer*—it would be
unbearable to have to accept them as genuine.   For in
these the poet, while praying for the forgiveness of sins,
is made specially to entreat the Divine pardon for his
" translations and inditing in worldly vanities," which he
" revokes in his retractions."   These include, besides the
Book of the Leo (doubtless a translation or adaptation
from Machault) and many other books which the
writer forgets, and " many a song and many a lecherous
lay," all the principal poetical works of Chaucer (with
the exception of the *Romaunt of the Rose*) discussed in
this essay.   On the other hand, he offers thanks for having

had the grace given him to compose his translation of
Boëthius and other moral and devotional works. There is,
to be sure, no actual evidence to decide in either way the
question as to the genuineness of this *Prayer*, which is
entirely one of internal probability. Those who will may
believe that the monks, who were the landlords of
Chaucer's house at Westminster, had in one way or the
other obtained a controlling influence over his mind.
Stranger things than this have happened ; but one prefers
to believe that the poet of the *Canterbury Tales* remained
master of himself to the last. He had written much
which a dying man might regret ; but it would be sad to
have to think that, " because of humility," he bore false
witness at the last against an immortal part of himself—
his poetic genius.

CHAPTER III.

THUS, then, Chaucer had passed away;—whether in good or in evil odour with the powerful interest with which John of Gaunt's son had entered into his unwritten concordate, after all matters but little now. He is no dim shadow to us, even in his outward presence; for we possess sufficient materials from which to picture to ourselves with good assurance what manner of man he was. Occleve painted from memory, on the margin of one of his own works, a portrait of his "worthy master," over against a passage in which, after praying the Blessed Virgin to intercede for the eternal happiness of one who had written so much in her honour, he proceeds as follows :—

> Although his life be quenched, the résemblance
> Of him hath in me so fresh liveliness,
> That to put other men in rémembrance
> Of his persón I have here his likenéss
> Made, to this end in very soothfastness,
> That they that have of him lost thought and mind
> May by the painting here again him find.

In this portrait, in which the experienced eye of Sir Harris Nicolas sees "incomparably the best portrait of Chaucer yet discovered," he appears as an elderly rather than aged man, clad in dark gown and hood—the latter

of the fashion so familiar to us from this very picture,
and from the well known one of Chaucer's last patron,
King Henry IV. His attitude in this likeness is that
of a quiet talker, with downcast eyes, but sufficiently erect
bearing of body. One arm is extended, and seems to be
gently pointing some observation which has just issued
from the poet's lips. The other holds a rosary, which
may be significant of the piety attributed to Chaucer by
Occleve, or may be a mere ordinary accompaniment of
conversation, as it is in parts of Greece to the present
day. The features are mild but expressive, with just a
suspicion—certainly no more—of saturnine or sarcastic
humour. The lips are full, and the nose is what is
called good by the learned in such matters. Several
other early portraits of Chaucer exist, all of which are
stated to bear much resemblance to one another. Among
them is one in an early if not contemporary copy of
Occleve's poems, full-length, and superscribed by the
hand which wrote the manuscript. In another, which is
extremely quaint, he appears on horseback, in commemo-
ration of his ride to Canterbury, and is represented as
short of stature, in accordance with the description of
himself in the *Canterbury Tales.*

For, as it fortunately happens, he has drawn his likeness for us with his own hand, as he appeared on the
occasion to that most free-spoken of observers and most
personal of critics, the host of the Tabard, the " cock " and
marshal of the company of pilgrims. The fellow-travellers
had just been wonderfully sobered (as well they might
be) by the piteous tale of the Prioress concerning the
little clergy-boy,—how, after the wicked Jews had cut his
throat because he ever sang *O Alma Redemptoris,* and
had cast him into a pit, he was found there by his mother

loudly giving forth the hymn in honour of the Blessed
Virgin which he had loved so well.   Master Harry Bailly
was, as in duty bound, the first to interrupt by a string of
jests the silence which had ensued :—

> And then at first he lookèd upon me,
> And saidè thus : " What man art thou ?" quoth he ;
> " Thou lookèst as thou wouldèst find a hare,
> For ever upon the ground I see thee stare.
> Approach more near, and lookè merrily !
> Now 'ware you, sirs, and let this man have space.
> He in the waist is shaped as well as I ;
> This were a puppet in an arm to embrace
> For any woman, small and fair of face.
> He seemeth elfish by his countenance,
> For unto no wight doth he dalliánce.

From this passage we may gather, not only that Chaucer
was, as the *Host* of the Tabard's transparent self-irony
implies, small of stature and slender, but that he was
accustomed to be twitted on account of the abstracted or
absent look which so often tempts children of the world
to offer its wearer a penny for his thoughts.   For " elfish "
means bewitched by the elves, and hence vacant or
absent in demeanour.

It is thus, with a few modest but manifestly truthful
touches, that Chaucer, after the manner of certain great
painters, introduces his own figure into a quiet corner of
his crowded canvas.   But mere outward likeness is of
little moment, and it is a more interesting enquiry whether
there are any personal characteristics of another sort, which
it is possible with safety to ascribe to him, and which
must be, in a greater or less degree, connected with
the distinctive qualities of his literary genius.   For in
truth it is but a sorry makeshift of literary biographers
to seek to divide a man who is an author into two separate

L

beings, in order to avoid the conversely fallacious procedure of accounting for everything which an author has written by something which the *man* has done or been inclined to do. What true poet has sought to hide, or succeeded in hiding, his moral nature from his muse? None in the entire band, from Petrarch to Villon, and least of all the poet whose song, like so much of Chaucer's, seems freshly derived from Nature's own inspiration.

One very pleasing quality in Chaucer must have been his modesty. In the course of his life this may have helped to recommend him to patrons so many and so various, and to make him the useful and trustworthy agent that he evidently became for confidential missions abroad. Physically, as has been seen, he represents himself as prone to the habit of casting his eyes on the ground ; and we may feel tolerably sure that to this external manner corresponded a quiet, observant disposition, such as that which may be held to have distinguished the greatest of Chaucer's successors among English poets. To us, of course, this quality of modesty in Chaucer makes itself principally manifest in the opinion which he incidentally shows himself to entertain concerning his own rank and claims as an author. Herein, as in many other points, a contrast is noticeable between him and the great Italian masters, who were so sensitive as to the esteem in which they and their poetry were held. Who could fancy Chaucer crowned with laurel, like Petrarch, or even, like Dante, speaking with proud humility of " the beautiful style that has done honour to him," while acknowledging his obligation for it to a great predecessor? Chaucer again and again disclaims all boasts of perfection, or pretensions to pre-eminence, as a poet. His Canterbury Pilgrims have in his name to

disavow, like Persius, having slept on Mount Parnassus,
or possessing "rhetoric" enough to describe a heroine's
beauty; and he openly allows that his spirit grows dull
as he grows older, and that he finds a difficulty as a
translator in matching his rhymes to his French original.
He acknowledges as incontestable the superiority of the
poets of classical antiquity :—

> —— Little book, no writing thou envý,
> But subject be to all true poësy,
> And kiss the steps, where'er thou seest space
> Of Virgil, Ovid, Homer, Lucan, Stace.[1]

But more than this. In the *House of Fame* he expressly
disclaims having in his light and imperfect verse sought
to pretend to "mastery" in the art poetical; and in a
charmingly expressed passage of the *Prologue* to the *Legend
of Good Women* he describes himself as merely following
in the wake of those who have already reaped the harvest
of amorous song, and have carried away the corn:—

> And I come after, gleaning here and there,
> And am full glad if I can find an ear
> Of any goodly word that ye have left.

Modesty of this stamp is perfectly compatible with a
certain self-consciousness which is hardly ever absent from
greatness, and which at all events supplies a stimulus not
easily dispensed with except by sustained effort on the part
of a poet. The two qualities seem naturally to combine
into that self-containedness (very different from self-con-
tentedness) which distinguishes Chaucer, and which helps
to give to his writings a manliness of tone, the direct opposite
of the irretentive querulousness found in so great a number
of poets in all times. He cannot indeed be said to

[1] Statius.

L 2

maintain an absolute reserve concerning himself and his
affairs in his writings ; but as he grows older, he seems to
become less and less inclined to take the public into his
confidence, or to speak of himself except in a pleasantly
light and incidental fashion.   And in the same spirit he
seems, without ever folding his hands in his lap, or
ceasing to be a busy man and an assiduous author, to
have grown indifferent to the lack of brilliant success in
life, whether as a man of letters or otherwise.   So at
least one seems justified in interpreting a remarkable
passage in the *House of Fame*, the poem in which
perhaps Chaucer allows us to see more deeply into his
mind than in any other.   After surveying the various
company of those who had come as suitors for the favours
of Fame, he tells us how it seemed to him (in his long
December dream) that some one spoke to him in a kindly
way,

> And saidë : " Friend, what is thy name ?
> Art thou come hither to have fame ? "
> " Nay, forsoothë, friend ! " quoth I ;
> " I came not hither (grand merci !)
> For no such causë, by my head !
> Sufficeth me, as I were dead,
> That no wight have my name in hand.
> I wot myself best how I stand ;
> For what I suffer, or what I think,
> I will myselfë all it drink,
> Or at least the greater part
> As far forth as I know my art."

With this modest but manly self-possession we shall
not go far wrong in connecting what seems another very
distinctly marked feature of Chaucer's inner nature.   He
seems to have arrived at a clear recognition of the truth
with which Goethe humorously comforted Eckermann in
the shape of the proverbial saying, " Care has been taken

that the trees shall not grow into the sky." Chaucer's, there is every reason to believe, was a contented faith, as far removed from self-torturing unrest as from childish credulity. Hence his refusal to trouble himself, now that he has arrived at a good age, with original research as to the constellations. (The passage is all the more significant since Chaucer, as has been seen, actually possessed a very respectable knowledge of astronomy.) That winged encyclopædia, the Eagle, has just been regretting the poet's unwillingness to learn the position of the Great and the Little Bear, Castor and Pollux, and the rest, concerning which at present he does not know where they stand. But he replies, "No matter!

> —— It is no need;
> I trust as well (so God me speed!)
> Them that write of this mattér,
> As though I knew their places there.

Moreover, as he says (probably without implying any special allegorical meaning), they seem so bright that it would destroy my eyes to look upon them. Personal inspection, in his opinion, was not necessary for a faith which at some times may, and at others must, take the place of knowledge; for we find him, at the opening of the *Prologue* to the *Legend of Good Women*, in a passage the tone of which should not be taken to imply less than its words express, writing as follows :—

> A thousand timës I have heard men tell,
> That there is joy in heaven, and pain in hell;
> And I accordë well that it is so.
> But nathëless, yet wot I well alsó,
> That there is none doth in this country dwell
> That either hath in heaven been or hell,
> Or any other way could of it know,
> But that he heard, or found it written so,

> For by assay may no man proof receive.
>   But God forbid that men should not believe
> More things than they have ever seen with eye !
> Men shall not fancy everything a lie
> Unless themselves it see, or else it do ;
> For, God wot, not the less a thing is true,
> Though every wight may not it chance to see.

The central thought of these lines, though it afterwards
receives a narrower and more commonplace application,
is no other than that which has been so splendidly
expressed by Spenser in the couplet :—

> Why then should witless man so much misween
> That nothing is but that which he hath seen ?

The *negative* result produced in Chaucer's mind by this
firm but placid way of regarding matters of faith was a
distrust of astrology, alchemy, and all the superstitions
which in the *Parson's Tale* are noticed as condemned by
the Church. This distrust on Chaucer's part requires no
further illustration after what has been said elsewhere ; it
would have been well for his age if all its children had
been as clear-sighted in these matters as he, to whom the
practices connected with these delusive sciences seemed,
and justly so from his point of view, not less impious
than futile. His *Canon Yeoman's Tale*, a story of impos-
ture so vividly dramatic in its catastrophe as to have suggested to Ben Jonson one of the most effective passages
in his comedy *The Alchemist*, concludes with a moral of
unmistakeable solemnity against the sinfulness, as well as
uselessness, of "multiplying" (making gold by the arts of
alchemy) :—

> —— Whoso maketh God his adversáry,
> As for to work anything in contràry
> Unto His will, certes ne'er shall he thrive,
> Though that he multiply through all his life.

But equally unmistakeable is the *positive* side of this
frame of mind in such a passage as the following—which
is one of those belonging to Chaucer himself, and not
taken from his French original—in *The Man of Law's Tale*.
The narrator is speaking of the voyage of Constance, after
her escape from the massacre in which, at a feast, all her
fellow-Christians had been killed, and of how she was
borne by the " wild wave" from " Surrey" (Syria) to the
Northumbrian shore :—

> Here men might askë, why she was not slain ?
> Eke at the feast who might her body save ?
> And I answérë that demand again :
> Who savèd Daniel in th' horríble cave,
> When every wight save him, master or knave,
> The lion ate—before he could depart ?
> No wight but God, whom he bare in his heart.

" In her," he continues, " God desired to show His miraculous power, so that we should see His mighty works.
For Christ, in whom we have a remedy for every ill, often
by means of His own does things for ends of His own,
which are obscure to the wit of man, incapable by reason
of our ignorance of understanding His wise providence.
But since Constance was not slain at the feast, it might be
asked : who kept her from drowning in the sea ?   Who,
then, kept Jonas in the belly of the whale, till he was
spouted up at Ninive ?   Well do we know it was no one
but He who kept the Hebrew people from drowning in
the waters, and made them to pass through the sea with
dry feet.   Who bade the four spirits of the tempest, which
have the power to trouble land and sea, north and south,
and west and east, vex neither sea nor land nor the trees
that grow on it ?   Truly these things were ordered by
Him who kept this woman safe from the tempest, as well

when she awoke as when she slept. But whence might this woman have meat and drink, and how could her sustenance last out to her for three years and more? Who, then, fed Saint Mary the Egyptian in the cavern or in the desert? Assuredly no one but Christ. It was a great miracle to feed five thousand folk with five loaves and two fishes; but God in their great need sent to them abundance."

As to the sentiments and opinions of Chaucer, then, on matters such as these, we can entertain no reasonable doubt. But we are altogether too ill acquainted with the details of his personal life, and with the motives which contributed to determine its course, to be able to arrive at any valid conclusions as to the way in which his principles affected his conduct. Enough has been already said concerning the attitude seemingly observed by him towards the great public questions, and the great historical events, of his day. If he had strong political opinions of his own, or strong personal views on questions either of ecclesiastical policy or of religious doctrine — in which assumptions there seems nothing probable — he at all events did not wear his heart on his sleeve, or use his poetry, allegorical or otherwise, as a vehicle of his wishes, hopes, or fears on these heads. The true breath of freedom could hardly be expected to blow through the precincts of a Plantagenet court. If Chaucer could write the pretty lines in the *Manciple's Tale* about the caged bird and its uncontrollable desire for liberty, his contemporary Barbour could apostrophise Freedom itself as a noble thing, in words the simple manliness of which stirs the blood after a very different fashion. Concerning his domestic relations, we may regard it as virtually certain that he was unhappy as a husband, though tender and affectionate as a father.

Considering how vast a proportion of the satire of all
times—but more especially that of the Middle Ages, and in
these again pre-eminently of the period of European literature which took its tone from Jean de Meung—is directed
against woman and against married life, it would be difficult to decide how much of the irony, sarcasm, and fun
lavished by Chaucer on these themes is due to a fashion with
which he readily fell in, and how much to the impulse of
personal feeling. A perfect anthology, or perhaps one should
rather say a complete herbarium, might be collected from
his works of samples of these attacks on women. He has
manifestly made a careful study of their ways, with which
he now and then betrays that curiously intimate acquaintance to which we are accustomed in a Richardson or a
Balzac. How accurate are such incidental remarks as this,
that women are " full measurable" in such matters as sleep
—not caring for so much of it at a time as men do ! How
wonderfully natural is the description of Cressid's bevy of
lady-visitors, attracted by the news that she is shortly to be
surrendered to the Greeks, and of the "nice vanity"—
i. e. foolish emptiness—of their consolatory gossip. "As
men see in town, and all about, that women are accustomed
to visit their friends," so a swarm of ladies came to Cressid,
"and sat themselves down, and said as I shall tell. ' I
am delighted,' says one, ' that you will so soon see your
father.' ' Indeed I am not so delighted,' says another, ' for
we have not seen half enough of her since she has been at
Troy.' ' I do hope,' quoth the third, ' that she will bring
us back peace with her ; in which case may Almighty God
guide her on her departure.' And Cressid heard these
words and womanish things as if she were far away ; for
she was burning all the time with another passion than any
of which they knew ; so that she almost felt her heart die

for woe, and for weariness of that company." But his
satire against women is rarely so innocent as this; and
though several ladies take part in the Canterbury Pilgrimage, yet pilgrim after pilgrim has his saw or jest
against their sex. The courteous *Knight* cannot refrain
from the generalisation that women all follow the favour
of fortune. The *Summoner*, who is of a less scrupulous
sort, introduces a diatribe against women's passionate love
of vengeance; and the *Shipman* seasons a story which
requires no such addition by an enumeration of their
favourite foibles. But the climax is reached in the con-
fessions of the *Wife of Bath*, who quite unhesitatingly says
that women are best won by flattery and busy attentions;
that when won they desire to have the sovereignty over their
husbands, and that they tell untruths and swear to them
with twice the boldness of men;—while as to the power of
their tongue, she quotes the second-hand authority of her
fifth husband for the saying that it is better to dwell with
a lion or a foul dragon, than with a woman accustomed
to chide. It is true that this same *Wife of Bath* also
observes with an effective *tu quoque*:—

> By God, if women had but written stories,
> As clerkës have within their oratòries,
> They would have writ of men more wickednéss
> Than all the race of Adam may redress;

and the *Legend of Good Women* seems, in point of fact,
to have been intended to offer some such kind of amends
as is here declared to be called for. But the balance still
remains heavy against the poet's sentiments of gallantry
and respect for women. It should at the same time be
remembered that among the *Canterbury Tales* the two
which are of their kind the most effective, constitute
tributes to the most distinctively feminine and wifely

virtue of fidelity.   Moreover, when coming from such personages as the pilgrims who narrate the *Tales* in question,
the praise of women has special significance and value.
The *Merchant* and the *Shipman* may indulge in facetious
or coarse jibes against wives and their behaviour, but the
Man of Law, full of grave experience of the world, is a
witness above suspicion to the womanly virtue of which
his narrative celebrates so illustrious an example, while the
Clerk of Oxford has in his cloistered solitude, where all
womanly blandishments are unknown, come to the conclusion that

> Men speak of Job, most for his humbleness,
> As clerkës, when they list, can well indite,
> Of men in special ; but, in truthfulness,
> Though praise by clerks of women be but slight,
> No man in humbleness can him acquit
> As women can, nor can be half so true
> As women are, unless all things be new.

As to marriage, Chaucer may be said generally to treat it
in that style of laughing with a wry mouth, which has
from time immemorial been affected both in comic writing
and on the comic stage, but which, in the end, even the
most determined old bachelor feels an occasional inclination to consider monotonous.

In all this, however, it is obvious that something at
least must be set down to conventionality. Yet the best part
of Chaucer's nature, it is hardly necessary to say, was
neither conventional nor commonplace.   He was not, we
may rest assured, one of that numerous class which in his
days, as it does in ours, composed the population of the
land of Philistia—the persons so well defined by the
Scottish poet, Sir David Lyndsay (himself a courtier of
the noblest type) :—

> Who fixèd have their hearts and whole intents
> On sensual lust, on dignity, and rents.

Doubtless Chaucer was a man of practical good sense,
desirous of suitable employment and of a sufficient in-
come ; nor can we suppose him to have been one of those
who look upon social life and its enjoyments with a jaun-
diced eye, or who, absorbed in things which are not of
this world, avert their gaze from it altogether.   But it is
hardly possible that rank and position should have been
valued on their own account by one who so repeatedly
recurs to his ideal of the true gentleman, as to a conception
dissociated from mere outward circumstances, and more
particularly independent of birth or inherited wealth.
At times, we know, men find what they seek ; and so
Chaucer found in Boëthius and in Guillaume de Lorris
that conception which he both translates and reproduces,
besides repeating it in a little *Ballade*, probably written by
him in the last *decennium* of his life.   By far the best-
known and the finest of these passages is that in the *Wife
of Bath's Tale*, which follows the round assertion that
the " arrogance" against which it protests is not worth
a hen ; and which is followed by an appeal to a parallel
passage in Dante :—

> Look, who that is most virtuous alway
> Privy and open, and most intendeth aye
> To do the gentle deedës that he can,
> Take him for the greatest gentleman.
> Christ wills we claim of Him our gentleness,
> Not of our elders for their old richés..
> For though they give us all their heritáge
> Through which we claim to be of high paráge,
> Yet may they not bequeathë for no thing—
> To none of us—their virtuous living,
> That made them gentlemen y-callèd be,
> And bade us follow them in such degree.

> Well can the wisë poet of Florénce,
> That Dante hightë, speak of this senténce;
> Lo, in such manner of rhyme is Dante's tale:
> " Seldom upriseth by its branches small
> Prowess of man; for God of His prowéss
> Wills that we claim of Him our gentleness;
> For of our ancestors we no thing claim
> But temporal thing, that men may hurt and maim."[1]

By the still ignobler greed of money for its own sake there is no reason whatever to suppose Chaucer to have been at any time actuated; although, under the pressure of immediate want, he devoted a *Complaint* to his empty purse, and made known, in the proper quarters, his desire to see it refilled.   Finally, as to what is commonly called pleasure, he may have shared the fashions and even the vices of his age; but we know hardly anything on the subject, except that excess in wine, which is often held a pardonable peccadillo in a poet, receives his emphatic condemnation. It would be hazardous to assert of him, as Herrick asserted of himself, that though his " Muse was jocund, his life was chaste;" inasmuch as his name occurs in one unfortunate connexion full of suspiciousness.   But we may at least believe him to have spoken his own sentiments in the Doctor of Physic's manly declaration that

> —— of all treason sovereign pestilence
> Is when a man betrayeth innocence.

---

[1] The passage in Canto viii. of the *Purgatorio* is thus translated by Longfellow:

> " Not oftentimes upriseth through the branches
> The probity of man; and this He wills
> Who gives it, so that we may ask of Him."

Its intention is only to show that the son is not necessarily what the father is before him; thus, Edward I. of England is a mightier man than was his father Henry III. Chaucer has ingeniously, though not altogether legitimately, pressed the passage into his service.

His true pleasures lay far away from those of vanity
and dissipation.   In the first place, he seems to have been
a passionate reader.   To his love of books he is constantly
referring; indeed, this may be said to be the only kind of
egotism which he seems to take a pleasure in indulging.
At the opening of his earliest extant poem of consequence,
the *Book of the Duchess*, he tells us how he preferred to
drive away a night rendered sleepless through melancholy
thoughts, by means of a book, which he thought better
entertainment than a game either at chess or at " tables."
This passion lasted longer with him than the other passion
which it had helped to allay ; for in the sequel to the
well-known passage in the *House of Fame*, already cited,
he gives us a glimpse of himself at home, absorbed in his
favourite pursuit :—

> Thou go'st home to thy house anon,
> And there, as dumb as any stone,
> Thou sittest at another book,
> Till fully dazèd is thy look;
> And liv'st thus as a hermit quite,
> Although thy abstinence is slight.

And doubtless he counted the days lost in which he was
prevented from following the rule of life which elsewhere
he sets himself, " to study and to read alway, day by day,"
and pressed even the nights into his service when he was
not making his head ache with writing.   How eager
and, considering the times in which he lived, how diverse
a reader he was, has already been abundantly illustrated
in the course of this volume.   His knowledge of Holy Writ
was considerable, though it probably for the most part
came to him at second-hand.   He seems to have had
some acquaintance with patristic and homiletic literature ;
he produced a version of the homily on Mary Magdalene,

improperly attributed to Origen; and, as we have seen, emulated King Alfred in translating Boëthius's famous manual of moral philosophy. His Latin learning extended over a wide range of literature, from Virgil and Ovid down to some of the favourite Latin poets of the Middle Ages. It is to be feared that he occasionally read Latin authors with so eager a desire to arrive at the contents of their books that he at times mistook their meaning—not far otherwise, slightly to vary a happy comparison made by one of his most eminent commentators, than many people read Chaucer's own writings now-a-days. That he possessed any knowledge at all of Greek may be doubted, both on general grounds and on account of a little slip or two in quotation of a kind not unusual with those who quote what they have not previously read. His *Troilus and Cressid* has only a very distant connexion indeed with Homer, whose *Iliad*, before it furnished materials for the mediæval Troilus-legend, had been filtered through a brief Latin epitome, and diluted into a Latin novel, and a journal kept at the seat of war, of altogether apocryphal value. And, indeed, it must in general be conceded that, if Chaucer had read much, he lays claim to having read more; for he not only occasionally ascribes to known authors works which we can by no means feel certain as to their having written, but at times he even cites (or is made to cite in all the editions of his works, authors who are altogether unknown to fame by the names which he gives to them. But then it must be remembered that other mediæval writers have rendered themselves liable to the same kind of charge. Quoting was one of the dominant literary fashions of the age; and just as a word without an oath went for but little in conversation, so a statement or sentiment in writing acquired a greatly enhanced value when suggested by authority, even after no more precise a fashion than the use of the phrase "as old books say." In Chaucer's days the equivalent of the modern "I have seen it said *somewhere*"—with perhaps the venturesome addition: "I *think*, in Horace"—had clearly not become an objectionable expletive.

Of modern literatures there can be no doubt that Chaucer had made substantially his own, the two which could be of importance to him as a poet. His obligations to the French singers have probably been over-estimated—at all events if the view adopted in this essay be the correct one, and if the charming poem of the *Flower and the Leaf*, together with the lively, but as to its meaning not very transparent, so-called *Chaucer's Dream*, be denied admission among his genuine works. At the same time, the influence of the *Roman de la Rose* and that of the courtly poets, of whom Machault was the chief in France and Froissart the representative in England, are perceptible in Chaucer almost to the last, nor is it likely that he should ever have ceased to study and assimilate them. On the other hand, the extent of his knowledge of Italian literature has probably till of late been underrated in an almost equal degree. This knowledge displays itself not only in the imitation or adaptation of particular poems, but more especially in the use made of incidental passages and details. In this way his debts to Dante were especially numerous; and it is curious to find proofs so abundant of Chaucer's relatively close study of a poet with whose genius his own had so few points in common. Notwithstanding first appearances, it is an open question whether Chaucer had ever read Boccaccio's *Decamerone*, with which he may merely have had in common the sources of several of his *Canterbury Tales*. But as he certainly took

one of them from the *Teseide* (without improving it in
the process), and not less certainly, and adapted the *Filostrato* in his *Troilus and Cressid*, it is strange that he should
refrain from naming the author to whom he was more
indebted than to any one other for poetic materials.

But wide and diverse as Chaucer's reading fairly de-
serves to be called, the love of nature was even stronger
and more absorbing in him than the love of books. He
has himself, in a very charming passage, compared the
strength of the one and of the other of his predilections :—

> And as for me, though I have knowledge slight,
> In bookës for to read I me delight,
> And to them give I faith and full credénce,
> And in my heart have them in reverence
> So heartily, that there is gamë none
> That from my bookës maketh me be gone,
> But it be seldom on the holiday,—
> Save, certainly, when that the month of May
> Is come, and that I hear the fowlës sing,
> And see the flowers as they begin to spring,
> Farewell my book, and my devotión.

Undoubtedly the literary fashion of Chaucer's times is
responsible for part of this May-morning sentiment, with
which he is fond of beginning his poems (the Canterbury
pilgrimage is dated towards the end of April—but is not
April "messenger to May"?). It had been decreed that
flowers should be the badges of nations and dynasties,
and the tokens of amorous sentiment; the rose had its
votaries, and the lily, lauded by Chaucer's *Prioress* as
the symbol of the Blessed Virgin; while the daisy, which
first sprang from the tears of a forlorn damsel, in France
gave its name (*marguérite*) to an entire species of courtly
verse. The enthusiastic adoration professed by Chaucer,

M

in the *Prologue* to the *Legend of Good Women*, for the daisy, which he afterwards identifies with the good Alceste, the type of faithful wifehood, is of course a mere poetical figure. But there is in his use of these favourite literary devices, so to speak, a variety in sameness significant of their accordance with his own taste, and of the frank and fresh love of nature which animated him, and which seems to us as much a part of him as his love of books. It is unlikely that his personality will ever become more fully known than it is at present; nor is there anything in respect of which we seem to see so clearly into his inner nature, as with regard to these twin predilections, to which he remains true in all his works, and in all his moods. While the study of books was his chief passion, nature was his chief joy and solace; while his genius enabled him to transfuse what he read in the former, what came home to him in the latter was akin to that genius itself; for he at times reminds us of his own fresh Canace, whom he describes as looking so full of happiness during her walk through the wood at sunrise :—

> What for the season, what for the morning
> And for the fowlës that she heardë sing,
> For right anon she wistë what they meant
> Right by their song, and knew all their intent.

If the above view of Chaucer's character and intellectual tastes and tendencies be in the main correct, there will seem to be nothing paradoxical in describing his literary progress, so far as its *data* are ascertainable, as a most steady and regular one. Very few men awake to find themselves either famous or great of a sudden, and perhaps as few poets as other men, though it may be heresy against a venerable maxim to say so. Chaucer's works form a clearly recognisable

series of steps towards the highest achievement of which,
under the circumstances in which he lived and wrote, he
can be held to have been capable ; and his long and
arduous self-training, whether consciously or not directed
to a particular end, was of that sure kind from which
genius itself derives strength. His beginnings as a writer
were dictated, partly by the impulse of that imitative
faculty which, in poetic natures, is the usual precursor of
the creative, partly by the influence of prevailing tastes and
the absence of native English literary predecessors whom,
considering the circumstances of his life and the nature of
his temperament, he could have found it a congenial task
to follow. French poems were, accordingly, his earliest
models; but fortunately (unlike Gower, whom it is so
instructive to compare with Chaucer, precisely because
the one lacked that gift of genius which the other possessed) he seems at once to have resolved to make use for
his poetical writings of his native speech. In no way, therefore, could he have begun his career with so happy a
promise of its future, as in that which he actually chose.
Nor could any course so naturally have led him to introduce
into his poetic diction the French idioms and words already
used in the spoken language of Englishmen, more especially in those classes for which he in the first instance
wrote, and thus to confer upon our tongue the great benefit
which it owes to him. Again most fortunately, others
had already pointed the way to the selection for literary
use of that English dialect which was probably the most
suitable for the purpose ; and Chaucer as a Southern man
(like his *Parson of a Town*) belonged to a part of the
country where the old alliterative verse had long since
been discarded for classical and romance forms of versification. Thus the *Romaunt of the Rose* most suitably

opens his literary life—a translation in which there is
nothing original except an occasional turn of phrase, but
in which the translator finds opportunity for exercising
his powers of judgment by virtually re-editing the work
before him. And already in the *Book of the Duchess*,
though most unmistakeably a follower of Machault, he is
also the rival of the great French *trouvère*, and has advanced
in freedom of movement not less than in agreeableness of
form. Then, as his travels extended his acquaintance with
foreign literatures to that of Italy, he here found abundant
fresh materials from which to feed his productive powers,
and more elaborate forms in which to clothe their results;
while at the same time comparison, the kindly nurse of
originality, more and more enabled him to recast instead
of imitating, or encouraged him freely to invent. In *Troilus
and Cressid* he produced something very different from a
mere condensed translation, and achieved a work in which
he showed himself a master of poetic expression and sustained narrative; in the *House of Fame* and the *Assembly
of Fowls* he moved with freedom in happily contrived
allegories of his own invention; and with the *Legend of
Good Women* he had already arrived at a stage when he
could undertake to review, under a pleasant pretext, but
with evident consciousness of work done, the list of his
previous works. " He hath," he said of himself, " made
many a lay and many a thing." Meanwhile the labour
incidentally devoted by him to translation from the Latin,
or to the composition of prose treatises in the scholastic
manner of academical exercises, could but little affect his
general literary progress. The mere scholarship of youth,
even if it be the reverse of close and profound, is wont to
cling to a man through life and to assert its modest claims
at any season; and thus, Chaucer's school-learning exercised

little influence either of an advancing or of a retarding
kind upon the full development of his genius. Nowhere
is he so truly himself as in the masterpiece of his last
years. For the *Canterbury Tales*, in which he is at once
greatest, most original, and most catholic in the choice of
materials as well as in moral sympathies, bears the unmistakeable stamp of having formed the crowning labour
of his life—a work which death alone prevented him from
completing.

It may be said, without presumption, that such a general
view as this leaves ample room for all reasonable theories
as to the chronology and sequence, where these remain
more or less unsettled, of Chaucer's indisputably genuine
works. In any case, there is no poet whom, if only as an
exercise in critical analysis, it is more interesting to study
and re-study in connexion with the circumstances of his
literary progress. He still, as has been seen, belongs to
the Middle Ages, but to a period in which the noblest ideals
of these Middle Ages are already beginning to pale and
their mightiest institutions to quake around him ; in which
learning continues to be in the main scholasticism, the
linking of argument with argument, and the accumulation
of authority upon authority, and poetry remains to a
great extent the crabbedness of clerks or the formality of
courts. Again, Chaucer is mediæval in tricks of style and
turns of phrase ; he often contents himself with the tritest
of figures and the most unrefreshing of ancient devices, and
freely resorts to a mixture of names and associations belonging to his own times with others derived from other ages.
This want of literary perspective is a sure sign of mediæ-
valism, and one which has amused the world, or has jarred
upon it, since the Renascence taught men to study both
classical and biblical antiquity as realities, and not merely

as a succession of pictures or of tapestries on a wall.
Chaucer mingles things mediæval and things classical as
freely as he brackets King David with the philosopher
Seneca, or Judas Iscariot with the Greek "dissimulator"
Sinon.   His. Dido, mounted on a stout palfrey paper
white of hue, with a red-and-gold saddle embroidered
and embossed, resembles Alice Perrers in all her pomp
rather than the Virgilian queen.   Jupiter's eagle, the
poet's guide and instructor in the allegory of the *House
of Fame,* invokes "Saint Mary, Saint James," and
"Saint Clare" all at once; and the pair of lovers at
Troy sign their letters "*la vostre* T." and *la vostre C.*"
Anachronisms of this kind (of the danger of which,
by the way, to judge from a passage in the *Prologue*
to the *Legend of Good Women,* Chaucer would not
appear to have been wholly unconscious) are intrinsically
of very slight importance.   But the morality of Chaucer's
narratives is at times the artificial and overstrained morality of the Middle Ages, which, as it were, clutches hold
of a single idea to the exclusion of all others—a morality
which, when carried to its extreme consequences, makes
monomaniacs as well as martyrs, in both of which species,
occasionally perhaps combined in the same persons, the
Middle Ages abound.   The fidelity of Griseldis under the
trials imposed upon her by her, in point of fact, brutal
husband is the fidelity of a martyr to unreason.   The
story was afterwards put on the stage in the Elizabethan
age; and though even in the play of *Patient Grissil* (by
Chettle and others), it is not easy to reconcile the
husband's proceedings with the promptings of common
sense, yet the playwrights, with the instinct of their
craft, contrived to introduce some element of humanity
into his character and of probability into his conduct.

Again, the supra-chivalrous respect paid by Arviragus,
the Breton knight of the *Franklin's Tale*, to the sanctity
of his wife's word, seriously to the peril of his own
and his wife's honour, is an effort to which probably
even the Knight of La Mancha himself would have
proved unequal. It is not to be expected that Chaucer
should have failed to share some of the prejudices of his
times as well as to fall in with their ways of thought and
sentiment ; and though it is the *Prioress* who tells a
story against the Jews which passes the legend of Hugh of
Lincoln, yet it would be very hazardous to seek any irony
in this legend of bigotry. In general, much of that *naïveté*
which to modern readers seems Chaucer's most obvious
literary quality must be ascribed to the times in which he
lived and wrote. This quality is in truth by no means that
which most deeply impresses itself upon the observation
of any one able to compare Chaucer's writings with those
of his more immediate predecessors and successors. But
the sense in which the term *naïf* should be understood in
literary criticism is so imperfectly agreed upon among
us, that we have not yet even found an English equivalent
for the word.

To Chaucer's times, then, belongs much of what may at
first sight seem to include itself among the characteristics
of his genius ; while, on the other hand, there are to be distinguished from these the influences due to his training and
studies in two literatures—the French and the Italian.
In the former of these he must have felt at home, if not
by birth and descent, at all events by social connexion,
habits of life, and ways of thought, while in the latter
he, whose own country's was still a half-fledged literary
life, found ready to his hand masterpieces of artistic
maturity, lofty in conception, broad in bearing, finished

in form. There still remain, for summary review, the
elements proper to his own poetic individuality—those
which mark him out not only as the first great poet of
his own nation, but as a great poet for all times.

The poet must please; if he wishes to be successful and
popular, he must suit himself to the tastes of his public;
and even if he be indifferent to immediate fame, he must,
as belonging to one of the most impressionable, the most
receptive species of humankind, live in a sense *with*
and *for* his generation. To meet this demand upon his
genius, Chaucer was born with many gifts which he carefully and assiduously exercised in a long series of poetical
experiments, and which he was able felicitously to combine
for the achievement of results unprecedented in our literature. In readiness of descriptive power, in brightness
and variety of imagery, and in flow of diction, Chaucer
remained unequalled by any English poet, till he was sur-
passed—it seems not too much to say, in all three respects
—by Spenser. His verse, where it suits his purpose, glitters,
to use Dunbar's expression, as with fresh enamel, and its
hues are variegated like those of a Flemish tapestry. Even
where his descriptive enumerations seem at first sight
monotonous or perfunctory, they are in truth graphic and
true in their details, as in the list of birds in the *Assembly
of Fowls*, quoted in part on an earlier page of this essay,
and in the shorter list of trees in the same poem, which
is, however, in its general features imitated from Boccaccio. Neither King James I. of Scotland, nor Spenser,
who after Chaucer essayed similar *tours de force*, were
happier than he had been before them. Or we may refer
to the description of the preparations for the tournament
and of the tournament itself in the *Knight's Tale*, or to the
thoroughly Dutch picture of a disturbance in a farm-yard

in the *Nun's Priest's.*   The vividness with which Chaucer
describes scenes and events as if he had them before his
own eyes, was no doubt, in the first instance, a result of his
own imaginative temperament ; but one would probably
not go wrong in attributing the fulness of the use which he
made of this gift to the influence of his Italian studies—
more especially to those which led him to Dante, whose
multitudinous characters and scenes impress themselves
with so singular and immediate a definiteness upon the
imagination.   At the same time, Chaucer's resources seem
inexhaustible for filling up or rounding off his narratives
with the aid of chivalrous love or religious legend, by the
introduction of samples of scholastic discourse or devices
of personal or general allegory.   He commands, where
necessary, a rhetorician's readiness of illustration, and a
masque-writer's inventiveness, as to machinery ; he can
even (in the *House of Fame*) conjure up an elaborate but
self-consistent phantasmagory of his own, and continue it
with a fulness proving that his fancy would not be at a
loss for supplying even more materials than he cares to
employ.

But Chaucer's poetry derived its power to please from
yet another quality ; and in this he was the first of our
English poets to emulate the poets of the two literatures
to which in the matter of his productions, and in the
ornaments of his diction, he owed so much.   There is in
his verse a music which hardly ever wholly loses itself,
and which at times is as sweet as that in any English
poet after him.

This assertion is not one which is likely to be gainsaid
at the present day, when there is not a single lover of
Chaucer who would sit down contented with Dryden's
condescending mixture of censure and praise.   " The verse

of Chaucer," he wrote, " I confess, is not harmonious to us. They who lived with him, and some time after him, thought it musical; and it continues so, even in our judgment, if compared with the numbers of Lydgate and Gower, his contemporaries : there is a rude sweetness of a Scotch tune in it, which is natural and pleasing, though not perfect." At the same time, it is no doubt necessary, in order to verify the correctness of a less balanced judgment, to take the trouble, which, if it could but be believed, is by no means great, to master the rules and usages of Chaucerian versification. These rules and usages the present is not a fit occasion for seeking to explain.[1]

---

[1] It may, however, be stated that they only partially connect themselves with Chaucer's use of forms which are now obsolete— more especially of inflexions of verbs and substantives (including several instances of the famous final *e*), and contractions with the negative *ne* and other monosyllabic words ending in a vowel, of the initial syllables of words beginning with vowels or with the letter *h*. These and other variations from later usage in spelling and pronunciation—such as the occurrence of an *e* (sometimes sounded and sometimes not) at the end of words in which it is now no longer retained, and again the frequent accentuation of many words of French origin in their last syllable, as in French, and of certain words of English origin analogously—are to be looked for as a matter of course in a last writing in the period of our language in which Chaucer lived. He clearly foresaw the difficulties which would be caused to his readers by the variations of usage in spelling and pronunciation—variations to some extent rendered inevitable by the fact that he wrote in an English dialect which was only gradually coming to be accepted as the uniform language of English writers. Towards the close of his *Troilus and Cressid*, he thus addresses his "little book," in fear of the mangling it might undergo from scriveners who might blunder in the copying of its words, or from reciters who might maltreat its verse in the distribution of the accents :—

> And, since there is so great diversity
> In English, and in writing of our tongue,

With regard to the most important of them is it not
too much to say that instinct and experience will very

> I pray to God that none may míswrite thee
> Nor thee mismetre, for default of tongue,
> And wheresoe'er thou mayst be read or sung,
> That thou be understood, God I beseech.

But in his versification he likewise adopted certain other
practices which had no such origin or reason as those already
referred to. Among them were the addition, at the end of a line
of five accents, of an unaccented syllable; and the substitution,
for the first foot of a line either of four or of five accents, of a
single syllable. These deviations from a stricter system of
versification he doubtless permitted to himself, partly for the sake
of variety, and partly for that of convenience; but neither of
them is peculiar to himself, or of supreme importance for the
effect of his verse. In fact, he seems to allow as much in a passage
of his *House of Fame*, a poem written, it should, however, be
observed, in an easy-going form of verse (the line of four accents)
which in his later period Chaucer seems with this exception to
have invariably discarded. He here beseeches Apollo to make his
rhyme

> somewhat agreeáble,
> Though some verse fail in a sylláble.

But another of his usages—the misunderstanding of which has
more than anything else caused his art as a writer of verse to be
misjudged—seems to have been due to a very different cause.
To understand the real nature of the usage in question it is only
necessary to seize the principle of Chaucer's rhythm. Of this
principle it was well said many years ago by a most competent
authority—Mr. R. Horne—that it is "inseparable from a full or
fair exercise of the genius of our language in versification."
For though this usage in its full freedom was gradually again
lost to our poetry for a time, yet it was in a large measure
recovered by Shakspere and the later dramatists of our great
age, and has since been never altogether abandoned again—not
even by the correct writers of the Augustan period—till by the
favourites of our own times it is resorted to with a perhaps
excessive liberality. It consists simply in *slurring* over certain
final syllables – not eliding them or contracting them with the

speedily combine to indicate to an intelligent reader where
the poet has resorted to it. *Without* intelligence on the
part of the reader, the beautiful harmonies of Mr. Tenny-
son's later verse remain obscure; so that, taken in this
way the most musical of English verse may seem as
difficult to read as the most rugged; but in the former
case the lesson is learnt not to be lost again, in the latter
the tumbling is ever beginning anew, as with the rock of
Sisyphus.   There is nothing that can fairly be called
rugged in the verse of Chaucer.

And fortunately there are not many pages in this poet's
works devoid of lines or passages the music of which cannot
escape any ear, however unaccustomed it may be to his
diction and versification.   What is the nature of the art
at whose bidding ten monosyllables arrange themselves
into a line of the exquisite cadence of the following :—

> And she was fair, as is the rose in May?

Nor would it be easy to find lines surpassing in their
melancholy charm Chaucer's version of the lament of
Medea, when deserted by Jason,—a passage which makes
the reader neglectful of the English poet's modest hint
that the letter of the Colchian princess may be found
at full length in Ovid.   The lines shall be quoted *verbatim*,
though not *literatim;* and perhaps no better example, and
none more readily appreciable by a modern ear, could be
given than the fourth of them of the harmonious effect of
Chaucer's usage of *slurring*, referred to above :—

syllables following upon them, but passing over them lightly, so
that, without being inaudible, they may at the same time not
interfere with the rhythm or beat of the verse. This usage, by
adding to the variety, incontestably adds to the flexibility and
beauty of Chaucer's versification.

Why likèd thee my yellow hair to see
More than the boundès of mine honesty?
Why likèd me thy youth and thy fairnéss
And of thy tongue the infinite graciousness?
O, had'st thou in thy conquest dead y-bee(n),
Full myckle untruth had there died with thee.

Qualities and powers such as the above, have belonged
to poets of very various times and countries before and
after Chaucer. But in addition to these he most
assuredly possessed others, which are not usual among
the poets of our nation, and which, whencesoever
they had come to him personally, had not, before they
made their appearance in him, seemed indigenous to the
English soil. It would indeed be easy to misrepresent
the history of English poetry, during the period which
Chaucer's advent may be said to have closed, by ascribing
to it a uniformly solemn and serious, or even dark and
gloomy, character. Such a description would not apply to
the poetry of the period before the Norman Conquest,
though, in truth, little room could be left for the play of
fancy or wit in the hammered-out war-song, or in the
long-drawn scriptural paraphrase. Nor was it likely that
a contagious gaiety should find an opportunity of mani-
festing itself in the course of the versification of grave
historical chronicles, or in the tranquil objective reproduction of the endless traditions of British legend. Of the
popular songs belonging to the period after the Norman
Conquest, the remains which furnish us with direct or
indirect evidence concerning them hardly enable us to
form an opinion. But we know that (the cavilling spirit
of Chaucer's burlesque *Rhyme of Sir Thopas* notwithstanding) the efforts of English metrical romance in the
thirteenth and fourteenth centuries were neither few nor
feeble, although these romances were chiefly translations,

sometimes abridgments to boot—even the Arthurian cycle
having been only imported across the Channel, though it
may have thus come back to its original home.   There is
some animation in at least one famous chronicle in verse,
dating from about the close of the thirteenth century;
there is real spirit in the war-songs of Minot in the
middle of the fourteenth; and from about its beginnings
dates a satire full of broad fun concerning the jolly
life led by the monks.   But none of these works or of
those contemporary with them show that innate lightness
and buoyancy of tone, which seems to add wings to the art
of poetry.   Nowhere had the English mind found so real
an opportunity of poetic utterance in the days of Chaucer's
own youth as in Langland's unique work, national in its
allegorical form and in its alliterative metre; and nowhere
had this utterance been more stern and severe.

No sooner, however, has Chaucer made his appearance as
a poet, than he seems to show what mistress's badge he
wears, which party of the two that have at most times
divided among them a national literature and its representatives he intends to follow.   The burden of his song is " Si
douce est la marguérite:" he has learnt the ways of French
gallantry as if to the manner born, and thus becomes, as it
were without hesitation or effort, the first English love-
poet.   Nor—though in the course of his career his range of
themes, his command of materials, and his choice of forms
are widely enlarged—is the gay banner under which he has
ranged himself ever deserted by him.   With the exception
of the *House of Fame*, there is not one of his longer poems
of which the passion of love, under one or another of its
aspects, does not either constitute the main subject or (as
in the *Canterbury Tales*) furnish the greater part of the
contents.   It is as a love-poet that Gower thinks of Chaucer

when paying a tribute to him in his own verse; it is to the attacks made upon him in his character as a love-poet, and to his consciousness of what he has achieved as such, that he gives expression in the *Prologue* to the *Legend of Good Women*, where his fair advocate tells the God of Love :—

> The man hath servèd you of his cunníng,
> And furthered well your law in his writíng,
> All be it that he cannot well indite,
> Yet hath he made unlearnèd folk delight
> To servë you in praising of your name.

And so he resumes his favourite theme once more, to tell, as the *Man of Law* says, " of lovers up and down, more than Ovid makes mention of in his old *Epistles.*" This fact alone—that our first great English poet was also our first English love-poet, properly so called—would have sufficed to transform our poetic literature through his agency.

What, however, calls for special notice, in connexion with Chaucer's special poetic quality of gaiety and brightness, is the preference which he exhibits for treating the joyous aspects of this many-sided passion. Apart from the *Legend of Good Women*, which is specially designed to give brilliant examples of the faithfulness of women under circumstances of trial, pain, and grief, and from two or three of the *Canterbury Tales*, he dwells with consistent preference on the bright side of love, though remaining a stranger to its divine radiance, which shines forth so fully upon us out of the pages of Spenser. Thus, in the *Assembly of Fowls* all is gaiety and mirth, as indeed beseems the genial neighbourhood of Cupid's temple. Again, in *Troilus and Cressid*, the earlier and cheerful part of the love-story is that which he developes with unmistake-

able sympathy and enjoyment, and in his hands this part of
the poem becomes one of the, most charming poetic narratives of the birth and growth of young love, which our
literature possesses—a soft and sweet counterpart to the
consuming heat of Marlowe's unrivalled *Hero and Leander*.
With Troilus it was love at first sight—with Cressid a
passion of very gradual growth.   But so full of nature is
the narrative of this growth, that one is irresistibly reminded at more than one point of the inimitable creations
of the great modern master in the description of women's
love.   Is there not a touch of Gretchen in Cressid, retiring
into her chamber to ponder over the first revelation to her
of the love of Troilus?—

> Cressid arose, no longer there she stayed,
> But straight into her closet went anon,
> And set her down, as still as any stone,
> And every word gan up and down to wind,
> That he had said, as it came to her mind.

And is there not a touch of Clärchen in her—though with
a difference—when from her casement she blushingly
beholds her lover riding past in triumph :

> So like a man of armës and a knight
> He was to see, filled full of high prowéss,
> For both he had a body, and a might
> To do that thing, as well as hardiness ;
> And eke to see him in his gear him dress,
> So fresh, so young, so wieldly seemëd he,
> It truly was a heaven him for to see.
>
> His helm was hewn about in twenty places,
> That by a tissue hung his back behind,
> His shield was dashed with strokes of swords and maces,
> In which men mightë many an arrow find
> That piercëd had the horn and nerve and rind ;
> And aye the people cried : " Here comes our joy,
> And, next his brother, holder up of Troy."

Even in the very *Book of the Duchess*, the widowed
lover describes the maiden charms of his lost wife with so
lively a freshness as almost to make one forget that it is a
lost wife whose praises are being recorded.

The vivacity and joyousness of Chaucer's poetic temperament, however, show themselves in various other
ways besides his favourite manner of treating a favourite
theme. They enhance the spirit of his passages of dialogue,
and add force and freshness to his passages of description.
They make him amusingly impatient of epical lengths,
abrupt in his transitions, and anxious, with an anxiety
usually manifested by readers rather than by writers, to
come to the point, " to the great effect," as he is wont to
call it. " Men," he says, " may overlade a ship or barge,
and therefore I will skip at once to the effect, and let all
the rest slip." And he unconsciously suggests a striking
difference between himself and the great Elizabethan epic
poet who owes so much to him, when he declines to make
as long a tale of the chaff or of the straw as of the corn,
and to describe all the details of a marriage-feast *seriatim :*

> The fruit of every tale is for to say :
> They eat and drink, and dance and sing and play.

This may be the fruit; but epic poets, from Homer downwards, have been generally in the habit of not neglecting
the foliage. Spenser in particular has that impartial copi-
ousness which we think it our duty to admire in the Ionic
epos, but which, if the truth were told, has prevented
generations of Englishmen from acquiring an intimate
personal acquaintance with the *Fairy Queen*. With
Chaucer the danger certainly rather lay in an opposite
direction. Most assuredly he can tell a story with
admirable point and precision, when he wishes to do so.

N

Perhaps no better example of his skill in this respect could
be cited than the *Manciple's Tale*, with its rapid narrative,
its major and minor catastrophe, and its concise moral,
ending thus :—

> My son, beware, and be no author new
> Of tidings, whether they be false or true ;
> Whereso thou comest, among high or low,
> Keep well thy tongue, and think upon the crow.

At the same time, his frequently recurring announcements
of his desire to be brief have the effect of making his
narrative appear to halt, and thus unfortunately defeat
their own purpose.   An example of this may be found in
the *Knight's Tale*, a narrative poem of which, in contrast
with its beauties, a want of evenness is one of the chief
defects.   It is not that the desire to suppress redundancies
is a tendency deserving anything but commendation in any
writer, whether great or small ; but rather, that the art of
concealing art had not yet dawned upon Chaucer. And yet,
few writers of any time have taken a more evident pleasure
in the process of literary production, and have more visibly
overflowed with sympathy for, or antipathy against, the
characters of their own creation.   Great novelists of our
own age have often told their readers, in prefaces to their
fictions or in *quasi*-confidential comments upon them, of
the intimacy in which they have lived with the offspring
of their own brain, to them far from shadowy beings.
But only the *naïveté* of Chaucer's literary age, together
with the vivacity of · his manner of thought and writing,
could place him in so close a personal relation towards the
personages and the incidents of his poems.   He is overcome by " pity and ruth " as he reads of suffering, and
his eyes " wax foul and sore " as he prepares to tell of
its infliction.   He compassionates " love's servants " as

if he were their own "brother dear;" and into his
adaptation of the eventful story of Constance (the *Man of
Law's Tale*) he introduces apostrophe upon apostrophe, to
the defenceless condition of his heroine—to her relentless
enemy the Sultana, and to Satan, who ever makes his
instrument of women "when he will beguile"—to the
drunken messenger who allowed the letter carried by him
to be stolen from him,—and to the treacherous Queen-
mother who caused them to be stolen.   Indeed, in address-
ing the last-named personage, the poet seems to lose all
control over himself.

> O Domegild, I have no English digne
> Unto thy malice and thy tyranny :
> And therefore to the fiend I thee resign,
> Let him at length tell of thy treachery.
> Fye, mannish, fye !—Oh nay, by God, I lie ;
> Fye fiendish spirit, for I dare well tell,
> Though thou here walk, thy spirit is in hell.

At the opening of the *Legend of Ariadne* he bids Minos
redden with shame ; and towards its close, when narrating
how Theseus sailed away, leaving his true-love behind, he
expresses a hope that the wind may drive the traitor " a
twenty devil way."   Nor does this vivacity find a less
amusing expression in so trifling a touch as that in the
Clerk's Tale, where the domestic sent to deprive Griseldis
of her boy becomes, *eo ipso* as it were, "this ugly ser-
geant."

Closely allied to Chaucer's liveliness and gaiety of disposition, and in part springing from them, are his keen
sense of the ridiculous and the power of satire which he
has at his command.   His humour has many varieties,
ranging from the refined and half-melancholy irony of the
House of Fame to the ready wit of the sagacious uncle of

N 2

Cressid, the burlesque fun of the inimitable *Nun's Priest's Tale*, and the very gross salt of the *Reeve*, the *Miller*, and one or two others. The springs of humour often capriciously refuse to allow themselves to be discovered ; nor is the satire of which the direct intention is transparent invariably the most effective species of satire. Concerning, however, Chaucer's use of the power which he in so large a measure possessed, viz. that of covering with ridicule the palpable vices or weaknesses of the classes or kinds of men represented by some of his character-types, one assertion may be made with tolerable safety. Whatever may have been the first stimulus and the ultimate scope of the wit and humour which he here expended, they are *not* to be explained as moral indignation in disguise. And in truth Chaucer's merriment flows spontaneously from a source very near the surface ; he is so extremely diverting, because he is so extremely diverted himself.

Herein, too, lies the harmlessness of Chaucer's fun. Its harmlessness, to wit, for those who are able to read him in something like the spirit in which he wrote— never a very easy achievement with regard to any author, and one which the beginner and the young had better be advised to abstain from attempting with Chaucer in the overflow of his more or less unrestrained moods. At all events, the excuse of gaiety of heart—the plea of that *vieil esprit Gaulois* which is so often, and very rarely without need, invoked in an exculpatory capacity by modern French criticism—is the best defence ever made for Chaucer's laughable irregularities, either by his apologists or by himself. "Men should not," he says, and says very truly, "make earnest of game." But when he audaciously defends himself against the charge of impropriety by declaring that he must tell stories *in character*, and coolly requests any person who may find anything in one of his tales objectionable to turn to another :—

> For he shall find enough, both great and small,
> Of storial thing that toucheth gentleness,
> Likewise morality and holiness ;
> Blame ye not me, if ye should choose amiss—

we are constrained to shake our heads at the transparent sophistry of the plea, which requires no exposure. For Chaucer knew very well how to give life and colour to his page without recklessly disregarding bounds the neglect of which was even in his day offensive to many besides the *"precious* folk" of whom he half derisively pretends to stand in awe. In one instance he defeated his own purpose ; for the so-called *Cook's Tale of Gamelyn* was substituted by some earlier editor for the original *Cook's Tale*, which has thus in its completed form become a rarity removed beyond the reach of even the most ardent of curiosity hunters. Fortunately, however, Chaucer spoke the truth when he said that from this point of view he had written very differently at different times ; no whiter pages remain than many of his.

But the realism of Chaucer is something more than exuberant love of fun and light-hearted gaiety. He is the first great painter of character, because he is the first great observer of it among modern European writers. His power of comic observation need not be dwelt upon again, after the illustrations of it which have been incidentally furnished in these pages. More especially with regard to the manners and ways of women, which often, while seeming so natural to women themselves, appear so odd to male observers, Chaucer's eye was ever on the alert. But

his works likewise contain passages displaying a penetrating insight into the minds of men, as well as a keen eye
for their manners, together with a power of generalising,
which, when kept within due bonds, lies at the root of the
wise knowledge of humankind so admirable to us in our
great essayists, from Bacon to Addison and his modern successors.   How truly, for instance, in *Troilus and Cressid,*
Chaucer observes on the enthusiastic belief of converts,
the " strongest-faithed " of men, as he understands !
And how fine is the saying as to the suspiciousness
characteristic of lewd, (i.e. ignorant,) people, that to things
which are made more subtly

> Than they can in their lewdness comprehend,

they gladly give the worst interpretation which suggests
itself !   How appositely the *Canon's Yeoman* describes
the arrogance of those who are too clever by half; "when
a man has an over-great wit," he says, " it very often
chances to him to misuse it " !   And with how ripe a
wisdom, combined with ethics of true gentleness, the
honest *Franklin*, at the opening of his *Tale*, discourses on
the uses and the beauty of long-suffering :—

> For one thing, sirës, safely dare I say,
> That friends the one the other must obey,
> If they will longë holdë company.
> Love will not be constrain'd by mastery.
> When mastery comes, the god of love anon
> Beateth his wings—and, farewell ! he is gone.
> Love is a thing as any spirit free.
> Women desire, by nature, liberty,
> And not to be constrainèd as a thrall,
> And so do men, if I the truth say shall.
> Look, who that is most patiént in love,
> He is at his advantage all above.
> A virtue high is patiénce, certaín,

Because it vanquisheth, as clerks explain,
Things to which rigour never could attain.
For every word men should not chide and plain;
Learn ye to suffer, or else, so may I go,
Ye shall it learn, whether ye will or no.
For in this world certaín no wight there is
Who neither doth nor saith some time amiss.
Sickness or ire, or constellatión,
Wine, woe, or changing of complexión,
Causeth full oft to do amiss or speak.
For every wrong men may not vengeance wreak:
After a time there must be temperance
With every wight that knows self-governance.

It was by virtue of his power of observing and drawing character, above all, that Chaucer became the true predecessor of two several growths in our literature, in both of which characterisation forms a most important element,— it might perhaps be truly said, the element which surpasses all others in importance. From this point of view the dramatic poets of the Elizabethan age remain unequalled by any other school or group of dramatists, and the English novelists of the eighteenth and nineteenth centuries by the representatives of any other development of prose-fiction. In the art of construction, in the invention and the arrangement of incident, these dramatists and novelists may have been left behind by others; in the creation of character they are on the whole without rivals in their respective branches of literature. To the earlier at least of these growths Chaucer may be said to have pointed the way. His personages, more especially of course, as has been seen, those who are assembled together in the *Prologue* to the *Canterbury Tales*, are not mere phantasms of the brain, or even mere actual possibilities, but real human beings, and types true to the likeness of whole classes of men and women, or to the mould in which all

human nature is cast. This is upon the whole the most
wonderful, as it is perhaps the most generally recognised,
of Chaucer's gifts. It would not of itself have sufficed to
make him a great dramatist, had the drama stood ready for
him as a literary form into which to pour the inspirations of
his genius, as it afterwards stood ready for our great Eliza-
bethans. But to it were added in him that perception
of a strong dramatic situation, and that power of finding
the right words for it, which have determined the success
of many plays, and the absence of which materially detracts
from the completeness of the effect of others, high as their
merits may be in other respects. How thrilling, for instance,
is that rapid passage across the stage, as one might almost
call it, of the unhappy Dorigen in the *Franklin's Tale !*
The antecedents of the situation, to be sure, are, as has
been elsewhere suggested, absurd enough ; but who can
fail to feel that spasm of anxious sympathy with which a
powerful dramatic situation in itself affects us, when the
wife, whom for truth's sake her husband has bidden be
untrue to him, goes forth on her unholy errand of duty?
" Whither so fast ?" asks the lover:

> And she made answer, half as she were mad :
> " Unto the garden, as my husband bade,
> My promise for to keep, alas ! alas ! "

Nor, as the abbreviated prose version of the *Pardoner's
Tale* given above will suffice to show, was Chaucer deficient
in the art of dramatically arranging a story ; while he is
not excelled by any of our non-dramatic poets in the
spirit and movement of his dialogue. The *Book of the
Duchess* and the *House of Fame*, but more especially
Troilus and Cressid and the connecting passages between
some of the *Canterbury Tales*, may be referred to in various
illustration of this.

The vividness of his imagination, which conjures up, so to speak, the very personality of his characters before him, and the contagious force of his pathos, which is as true and as spontaneous as his humour, complete in him the born dramatist. We can see Constance as with our own eyes, in the agony of her peril :—

> Have ye not seen some time a pallid face
> Among a press, of him that hath been led
> Towards his death, where him awaits no grace,
> And such a colour in his face hath had,
> Men mightë know his face was so bested
> 'Mong all the other faces in that rout ?
> So stands Constánce, and looketh her about.

And perhaps there is no better way of studying the general character of Chaucer's pathos, than a comparison of the *Monk's Tale* from which this passage is taken, and the *Clerk's Tale*, with their originals. In the former, for instance, the prayer of Constance, when condemned through Domegild's guilt to be cast adrift once more on the waters, her piteous words and tenderness to her little child, as it lies weeping in her arm, and her touching leave-taking from the land of the husband who has con-demned her,—all these are Chaucer's own. So also are parts of one of the most affecting passages in the *Clerk's Tale*—Griseldis' farewell to her daughter. But it is as unnecessary to lay a finger upon lines and passages illus-trating Chaucer's pathos, as upon others illustrating his humour.

Thus, then, Chaucer was a born dramatist; but fate willed it, that the branch of our literature which might probably have of all been the best suited to his genius was not to spring into life till he and several generations after him had passed away. To be sure, during the fourteenth century, the so-called miracle-plays flourished abundantly in England, and were, as there is every reason to believe, already largely performed by the trading-companies of London and the towns. The allusions in Chaucer to these beginnings of our English drama are, however, remarkably scanty. The *Wife of Bath* mentions plays of miracles among the other occasions of religious sensation haunted by her, clad in her gay scarlet gown,— including vigils, processions, preachings, pilgrimages, and marriages. And the jolly parish-clerk of the *Miller's Tale*, we are informed, at times, in order to show his lightness and his skill, played "Herod on a scaffold high"—thus, by the bye, emulating the parish clerks of London, who are known to have been among the performers of miracles in the Middle Ages. The allusion to Pilate's voice in the *Miller's Prologue*, and that in the *Tale* to

> The sorrow of Noah with his fellowship
> That he had ere he got his wife to ship,

seem likewise dramatic reminiscences ; and the occurrence of these three allusions in a single *Tale* and its *Prologue* would incline one to think that Chaucer had recently amused himself at one of these performances. But plays are not mentioned among the entertainments enumerated at the opening of the *Pardoner's Tale ;* and it would in any case have been unlikely that Chaucer should have paid much attention to diversions which were long chiefly "visited" by the classes with which he could have no personal connexion, and even at a much later date were dissociated in men's minds from poetry and literature. Had he ever written anything remotely partaking of the nature of a dramatic piece, it could at the most have been the words of the songs in some congratulatory royal

pageant such as Lydgate probably wrote on the return of
Henry V. after Agincourt; though there is not the least
reason for supposing Chaucer to have taken so much
interest in the "ridings" through the City which occupied
many a morning of the idle apprentice of the *Cook's Tale*,
Perkyn Revellour.   It is perhaps more surprising to find
Chaucer, who was a reader of several Latin poets, and
who had heard of more, both Latin and Greek, show no
knowledge whatever of the ancient classical drama, with
which he may accordingly be fairly concluded to have
been wholly unacquainted.

To one further aspect of Chaucer's realism as a poet
reference has already been made; but a final mention
of it may most appropriately conclude this sketch of his
poetical characteristics.   His descriptions of nature are as
true as his sketches of human character; and incidental
touches in him reveal his love of the one as unmistakeably
as his unflagging interest in the study of the other.   Even
these May-morning *exordia*, in which he was but following a fashion—faithfully observed both by the French
trouvères and by the English romances translated from
their productions, and not forgotten by the author of the
earlier part of the *Roman de la Rose*—always come from
his hands with the freshness of natural truth.   They
cannot be called original in conception, and it would be
difficult to point out in them anything strikingly original
in execution; yet they cannot be included among those
matter-of-course notices of morning and evening, sunrise
and sunset, to which so many poets have accustomed us
since (be it said with reverence) Homer himself.   In
Chaucer these passages make his page " as fresh as is the
month of May."   When he went forth on these April
and May mornings, it was not solely with the intent of

composing a roundelay or a *marguérite;* but we may be well
assured, he allowed the song of the little birds, the perfume of the flowers, and the fresh verdure of the English landscape, to sink into his very soul.   For nowhere
does he seem, and nowhere could he have been, more open
to the influence which he received into himself, and which
in his turn he exercised, and exercises, upon others, than
when he was in fresh contact with nature.   In this influence
lies the secret of his genius ; in his poetry there is *life.*

CHAPTER IV.

THE legacy which Chaucer left to our literature was to fructify in the hands of a long succession of heirs; and it may be said, with little fear of contradiction, that at no time has his fame been fresher and his influence upon our poets—and upon our painters as well as our poets—more perceptible than at the present day. When Gower first put forth his *Confessio Amantis,* we may assume that Chaucer's poetical labours, of the fame of which his brother-poet declared the land to be full, had not yet been crowned by his last and greatest work. As a poet, therefore, Gower in one sense owes less to Chaucer than did many of their successors; though, on the other hand it may be said with truth that to Chaucer is due the fact, that Gower (whose earlier productions were in French and in Latin) ever became a poet at all. The *Confessio Amantis* is no book for all times like the *Canterbury Tales;* but the conjoined names of Chaucer and Gower added strength to one another in the eyes of the generations ensuing, little anxious as these generations were to distinguish which of the pair was really the first to "garnish our English rude" with the flowers of a new poetic diction and art of verse.

The Lancaster peried of our history had its days of

national glory as well as of national humiliation, and
indisputably, as a whole, advanced the growth of the
nation towards political manhood. But it brought with
it no golden summer to fulfil the promises of the spring-
tide of our modern poetical literature. The two poets
whose names stand forth from the barren after-season of
the earlier half of the fifteenth century, were, both of
them, according to their own profession, disciples of
Chaucer. In truth, however, Occleve, the only name-
worthy poetical writer of the reign of Henry IV., seems
to have been less akin as an author to Chaucer than to
Gower, while his principal poem manifestly was, in an even
greater degree than the *Confessio Amantis*, a severely
learned or, as its author terms it, unbuxom book.
Lydgate, on the other hand, the famous monk of Bury,
has in him something of the spirit as well as of the manner of Chaucer, under whose advice he is said to have
composed one of his principal poems. Though a monk, he
was no stay-at-home or do-nothing; like him of the *Canterbury Tales*, we may suppose Lydgate to have scorned
the maxim that a monk out of his cloister is like a fish
out of water; and doubtless many days which he could
spare from the instruction of youth at St. Edmund's Bury
were spent about the London streets, of the sights and
sounds of which he has left us so vivacious a record—a
kind of farcical supplement to the *Prologue* of the *Canterbury Tales*. His literary career, part of which certainly
belongs to the reign of Henry V., has some resemblance to
Chaucer's, though it is less regular and less consistent with
itself; and several of his poems bear more or less distinct
traces of Chaucer's influence. The *Troy-book* is not
founded on *Troilus and Cressid*, though it is derived from
the sources which had fed the original of Chaucer's poem;

but the *Temple of Glass* seems to have been an imitation
of the *House of Fame;* and the *Story of Thebes* is actually
introduced by its author as an additional *Canterbury Tale,*
and challenges comparison with the rest of the series into
which it asks admittance. Both Occleve and Lydgate enjoyed the patronage of a prince of genius descended from
the House, with whose founder Chaucer was so closely
connected—Humphrey, Duke of Gloucester. Meanwhile,
the sovereign of a neighbouring kingdom was in all
probability himself the agent who established the influence of Chaucer as predominant in the literature
of his native land. The long though honourable captivity in England of King James I. of Scotland—
the best poet among kings and the best king among
poets, as he has been antithetically called—was con-
soled by the study of the "hymns" of his "dear masters, Chaucer and Gower," for the happiness of whose souls
he prays at the close of his poem, *The King's Quair*. That
most charming of love-allegories, in which the Scottish
king sings the story of his captivity and of his deliverance
by the sweet messenger of love, not only closely imitates
Chaucer in detail, more especially at its opening, but
is pervaded by his spirit. Many subsequent Scottish poets
imitated Chaucer, and some of them loyally acknowledged
their debts to him. Gawin Douglas in his *Palace of Honour*,
and Henryson in his *Testament of Cressid* and elsewhere, are followers of the southern master. The wise and
brave Sir David Lyndsay was familiar with his writings;
and he was not only occasionally imitated, but praised with
enthusiastic eloquence by William Dunbar, that "darling
of the Scottish Muses," whose poetical merits Sir Walter
Scott, from some points of view, can hardly be said to have
exaggerated, when declaring him to have been "justly

raised to a level with Chaucer by every judge of poetry, to
whom his obsolete language has not rendered him unin-
telligible." Dunbar knew that this Scottish language
was but a form of that which, as he declared, Chaucer
had made to " surmount every terrestrial tongue, as far
as midnight is surmounted by a May morning."

Meanwhile, in England, the influence of Chaucer continued to live even during the dreary interval which
separates from one another two important epochs of our
literary history. Now, as in the days of the Norman
kings, ballads orally transmittted were the people's
poetry ; and one of these popular ballads carried the story
of *Patient Grissel* into regions where Chaucer's name was
probably unknown. When, after the close of the troubled
season of the Roses, our poetic literature showed the first
signs of a revival, they consisted in a return to the old
masters of the fourteenth century. The poetry of Hawes,
the learned author of the crabbed *Pastime of Pleasure*,
exhibits an undeniable continuity with that of Chaucer,
Gower, and Lydgate, to which triad he devotes a chapter
of panegyric. Hawes, however, presses into the service
of his allegory not only all the Virtues and all the Vices,
whom from habit we can tolerate in such productions, but
also Astronomy, Geometry, Arithmetic, and the rest of
the seven Daughters of Doctrine, whom we *cannot;* and
is altogether inferior to the least of his models. It is at
the same time to his credit that he seems painfully aware
of his inability to cope with either Chaucer or Lydgate as
to vigour of invention. There is, in truth, more of the
dramatic spirit of Chaucer in Barklay's *Ship of Fools*,
which, though essentially a translation, achieved in England the popularity of an original work. For this poem,
like the *Canterbury Tales*, introduces into its admirable

framework a variety of lifelike sketches of character and
manners; it has in it that dramatic element which is so
Chaucerian a characteristic. But the aim of its author
was didactic, which Chaucer's had never been.

When with the poems of Surrey and Wyatt, and with
the first attempts in the direction of the regular drama,
the opening of the second great age in our literature approached, and when, about half a century afterwards, that
age actually opened with an unequalled burst of varied
productivity, it would seem as if Chaucer's influence might
naturally enough have passed away, or at least become
obscured. Such was not, however, the case, and Chaucer
survived into the age of the English Renascence as an established English classic, in which capacity Caxton had
honoured him by twice issuing an edition of his works
from the Westminster printing-press. Henry VIII.'s
favourite, the reckless but pithy satirist, Skelton, was
alive to the merits of his great predecessor, and Skelton's
patron, William Thynne, a royal official, busied himself with editing Chaucer's works. The loyal servant
of Queen Mary, the wise and witty John Heywood, from
whose *Interludes* the step is so short to the first regular
English comedy, in one of these pieces freely plagiarised
a passage in the *Canterbury Tales*. Tottel, the printer of
the favourite poetic *Miscellany* published shortly before
Queen Elizabeth's accession, included in his collection
the beautiful lines, cited above, called *Good Counsel of
Chaucer*. And when, at last, the Elizabethan era properly so-called began, the proof was speedily given that
geniuses worthy of holding fellowship with Chaucer had
assimilated into their own literary growth what was con-
gruous to it in his, just as he had assimilated to himself—
not always improving, but hardly ever merely borrowing

o

or taking over—much that he had found in the French
trouvères, and in Italian poetry and prose. The first work
which can be included in the great period of Elizabethan
literature is the *Shepherd's Calendar*, where Spenser is
still in a partly imitative stage; and it is Chaucer whom
he imitates and extols in his poem, and whom his *alter
ego*, the mysterious " *E. K.*," extols in preface and notes.
The longest of the passages in which reference is made by
Spenser to Chaucer, under the pseudonym of Tityrus, is
more especially noteworthy, both as showing the venera-
tion of the younger for the older poet, and as testifying
to the growing popularity of Chaucer at the time when
Spenser wrote.

The same great poet's debt to his revered predecessor
in the *Daphnaïda* has been already mentioned.   The
Fairy Queen is the masterpiece of an original mind,
and its supreme poetic quality is a lofty magnificence upon
the whole foreign to Chaucer's genius; but Spenser owed
something more than his archaic forms to "Tityrus,"
with whose style he had erst disclaimed all ambition to
match his pastoral pipe.   In a well-known passage of his
great epos he declares that it is through sweet infusion
of the older poet's own spirit that he, the younger, follows the footing of his feet, in order so the rather to meet
with his meaning.   It was this, the romantic spirit proper, which Spenser sought to catch from Chaucer, but
which, like all those who consciously seek after it, he trans-
muted into a new quality and a new power.   With
Spenser the change was into something mightier and
loftier.   He would, we cannot doubt, readily have echoed
the judgment of his friend and brother-poet concerning
Chaucer.   " I know not," writes Sir Philip Sidney,
" whether to marvel more, either that he in that misty

time could see so clearly, or that we, in this clear age, walk so stumblingly after him. Yet had he," adds Sidney with the generosity of a true critic, who is not lost in wonder at his own cleverness in discovering defects, "great wants, fit to be forgiven in so reverent an antiquity." And yet a third Elizabethan, Michael Drayton, pure of tone and high of purpose, joins his voice to those of Spenser and Sidney, hailing in the " noble Chaucer "

> —— the first of those that ever brake
> Into the Muses' treasure and first spake
> In weighty numbers,

and placing Gower, with a degree of judgment not reached by his and Chaucer's immediate successors, in his proper relation of poetic rank to his younger but greater contemporary.

To these names should be added that of George Puttenham—if he was indeed the author of the grave and elaborate treatise, dedicated to Lord Burghley, on *The Art of English Poësy*. In this work mention is repeatedly made of Chaucer, " father of our English poets ;" and his learning, and " the natural of his pleasant wit," are alike judiciously commended. One of Puttenham's best qualities as a critic is that he never speaks without his book ; and he comes very near to discovering Chaucer's greatest gift when noticing his excellence in *prosopographia*—a term which to Chaucer would perhaps have seemed to require translation. At the obsoleteness of Chaucer's own diction this critic, who writes entirely " for the better brought-up sort," is obliged to shake his learned head.

Enough has been said in the preceding pages to support the opinion that among the wants which fell to the lot of

Chaucer as a poet, perhaps the greatest (though Sidney would never have allowed this), was the want of poetic form most in harmony with his most characteristic gifts. The influence of Chaucer upon the dramatists of the Elizabethan age was probably rather indirect and general than direct and personal; but indications or illustrations of it may be traced in a considerable number of these writers, including perhaps among the earliest Richard Edwards as the author of a non-extant tragedy, *Palamon and Arcite*, and among the latest the author—or authors—of *The Two Noble Kinsmen*. Besides Fletcher and Shakspere, Greene, Nash and Middleton, and more especially Jonson (as both poet and grammarian), were acquainted with Chaucer's writings; so that it is perhaps rather a proof of the widespread popularity of the *Canterbury Tales* than the reverse, that they were not largely resorted to for materials by the Elizabethan and Jacobean dramatists. Under Charles I. *Troilus and Cressid* found a translator in Sir Francis Kynaston, whom Cartwright congratulated on having made it possible " that we read Chaucer now without a dictionary." A personage, however, in Cartwright's best known play, the Antiquary Moth, prefers to talk on his own account " genuine " Chaucerian English.

To pursue the further traces of the influence of Chaucer through such a literary aftergrowth as the younger Fletchers, into the early poems of Milton, would be beyond the purpose of the present essay. In the treasure-house of that great poet's mind were gathered memories and associations innumerable, though the sublimest flights of his genius soared aloft into regions whither the imagination of none of our earlier poets had preceded them.   On the other hand, the days have passed for attention to be spared for the treatment experienced by

Chaucer in the Augustan Age, to which he was a barba-
rian only to be tolerated if put into the court-dress
of the final period of civilisation. Still, even thus, he
was not left altogether unread ; nor was he in all cases
adapted without a certain measure of success. The irrepressible vigour, and the frequent felicity, of Dryden's
Fables contrast advantageously with the tame evenness
of the *Temple of Fame*, an early effort by Pope, who had
wit enough to imitate in a juvenile parody some of the
grossest peculiarities of Chaucer's manner, but who would
have been quite ashamed to reproduce him in a serious
literary performance, without the inevitable polish and
cadence of his own style of verse. Later modernisations
— even of those which a band of poets in some instances
singularly qualified for the task put forth in a collection
published in the year 1841, and which, on the part of some
of them at least, was the result of conscientious endeavour
— it is needless to characterise here. Slight incidental
use has been made of some of these in this essay, the
author of which would gladly have abstained from printing a single modernised phrase or word—most of all any
which he has himself been guilty of re-casting. The time
cannot be far distant when even the least unsuccessful of
such attempts will no longer be accepted, because no such
attempts whatever will be any longer required. No
Englishman or Englishwoman need go through a very
long or very laborious apprenticeship in order to become
able to read, understand, and enjoy what Chaucer himself
wrote. But if this apprenticeship be too hard, then some
sort of makeshift must be accepted, or antiquity must
remain the "canker-worm" even of a great national poet,
as Spenser said it had already in his day proved to be of
Chaucer.

Meanwhile, since our poetic literature has long thrown
off the shackles which forced it to adhere to one particular group of models, he is not a true English poet
who should remain uninfluenced by any of the really great
among his predecessors. If Chaucer has again, in a special
sense, become the " master dear and father reverent " of
some of our living poets, in a wider sense he must hold
this relation to them all and to all their successors, so long
as he continues to be known and understood. As it is,
there are few worthies of our literature whose names seem
to awaken thoughout the English-speaking world a readier
sentiment of familiar regard ; and in New England, where
the earliest great poet of Old England is cherished not
less warmly than among ourselves, a kindly cunning has
thus limned his likeness :—

> An old man in a lodge within a park ;
> The chamber walls depicted all around
> With portraiture of huntsman, hawk and hound,
> And the hurt deer. He listeneth to the lark,
> Whose song comes with the sunshine through the dark
> Of painted glass in leaden lattice bound ;
> He listeneth and he laugheth at the sound,
> Then writeth in a book like any clerk.
> He is the poet of the dawn, who wrote
> The Canterbury Tales, and his old age
> Made beautiful with song ; and as I read
> I hear the crowing cock, I hear the note
> Of lark and linnet, and from every page
> Rise odours of ploughed field or flowery mead.

GLOSSARY.

Bencite = benedicite.

Clepe, call.

Deem, judge.

Despitous, angry to excess.

Digne, fit ;— disdainful.

Frere, friar.

Gentle, well-born.

Keep, care.

Languor, grief.

Meinie, following, household.

Meet, mate (?), measure (?).

Overthwart, across.

Parage, rank, degree.

Press, crowd.

Rede, advise, counsel.

Reeve, steward, bailiff.

Ruth, pity.

Scall, scab.

Shapely, fit.

Sithe, time.

Spiced, nice, scrupulous.

Targe, target, shield.

Y prefix of past participle as in *y-bee* = *bee(n)*.

While, time ; *to quite his while* to reward his pains.

Wieldy, active.

Wone, custom, habit.

*** A dotted ë should always be sounded in reading.

THE END.

For EU product safety concerns, contact us at Calle de José Abascal, 56–1°,
28003 Madrid, Spain or eugpsr@cambridge.org.

www.ingramcontent.com/pod-product-compliance
Ingram Content Group UK Ltd.
Pitfield, Milton Keynes, MK11 3LW, UK
UKHW012346130625
459647UK00009B/578